I0438117

# GOING AFTER THE COWS

by

## Gary L Jackson

authorHOUSE®

*AuthorHouse™*
*1663 Liberty Drive, Suite 200*
*Bloomington, IN 47403*
*www.authorhouse.com*
*Phone: 1-800-839-8640*

*© 2008 Gary L Jackson. All rights reserved.*

*No part of this book may be reproduced, stored in a retrieval system, or transmitted by any means without the written permission of the author.*

*First published by AuthorHouse 2/5/2008*

*ISBN: 978-1-4343-4066-5 (sc)*

*Printed in the United States of America*
*Bloomington, Indiana*

*This book is printed on acid-free paper.*

# TABLE OF CONTENTS

# FOREWORD

Upon reaching middle-age, and having read a variety of histories and recollections about the "good ole days" or "growing up" I decided that the conditions of my childhood were worth recounting—for me if for no one else. The process of writing and revising has taken me twenty years.

The period of my childhood, 1938 to roughly 1954, (exactly when childhood ended and manhood started I do not remember) was one of tremendous change in a world that saw discoveries, among them nuclear fission, which irrevocably altered mankind's future. For agriculture this period saw the transition from horse power to tractor power. The economic and sociological changes which resulted from that transition greatly, and likely forever, changed the nature of farming and farm life in this country. I grew up on a farm in northwestern Missouri, thus these rambling recollections are about a childhood spent in a Midwestern farm community.

My memories were not recorded in strict chronological (and probably not logical) order, but rather in the order in which they came to mind and in which I felt ready to record them. Subsequently I reordered them into what I hope is a logical progression. In this process I attempted to describe the land, the conditions, some events and some of the wonderful people who enriched my life in those days. I also took the opportunity to share some lessons and thoughts about what I experienced.

I apologize to any who are, or who know or have known, any of the folks mentioned in these musings if I have portrayed them in less than a wholly flattering or favorable way. The reader should keep in mind that although memories recorded here have been diluted by the years, I attempted to honestly portray these decent people, most of whom had a positive influence on my life. My intent has been to produce a personal, "historically accurate," though admittedly incomplete record rather than a document for the entertainment of others. Still I hope that the reader will find these thoughts of interest and value—and perhaps be led to contemplate not only the past, but also the present and future.

Perhaps these records will culminate in a volume of interest to others. If not, they may become just a pile of old papers of interest to offspring or far distant historians or collectors who like to poke around bookcases or boxes of old papers. In any case I have enjoyed the process of remembering and writing. I titled the series *Going After The Cows* simply because it was the first title that came to mind.

# THE SETTING

MOST OF THE events recorded here occurred in Holt County, Missouri which is located in the northwestern part of the state. Holt County is bordered on the west by the Missouri River. Northern Kansas and southern Nebraska lie just across the river. Iowa is but one county, Atchison, to the north.

The Pennsylvanian limestone outcrops exposed along the bluffs in the southern part of Holt County provide incontrovertible evidence that the area once was covered by oceans. With little effort one can find the shells of ancient mussels and brachiopods embedded in the rock. The land then rose from the oceans, weathered for millions of years, and was covered, multiple times, by great ice sheets. Much later, but perhaps only as recently as ten thousand years ago, the ice of the last glacier receded leaving scattered gravel beds and the red rocks which the citizens of Mound City have gathered to decorate their town. Then great west winds gradually piled loess soils hundreds of feet deep. The mastodon and camel and other Pleistocene animals grazed the developing prairie and roamed the scattered forests. As the climate warmed these creatures were replaced by the bison, elk, deer and first human immigrants from the far east and north. Within recorded history my immediate ancestors came from across the Atlantic and gradually moved west. In July 1804, on their trip up the Missouri River, Lewis and Clark recorded camping in what was to become Holt County. The hunting party killed seven deer near the mouth of one of the tributaries—either the Little or Big Tarkio Creek where it enters the Missouri River from Holt County.

The Missouri River valley is five to ten miles wide here, thus endowing the county with some of the richest "bottom land" soils in the world. Until the late 1950s the river often flooded and the flood plain retained a mixture of forests and marshes interspersed with scattered farm fields. During the 1950s and 1960s the Army Corps of Engineers instituted an aggressive plan of flood control that led to additional drainage and clearing of the remaining bottom-land woods and their conversion to large grain fields.

The eastern and northeastern edges of the river valley are bordered by impressive bluffs composed of the bedrock Pennsylvanian limestone topped with deep wind-blown loess soil. In some areas, particularly that occupied by the Squaw Creek National Wildlife Refuge, the bluffs were sculpted into miniature mountains nearly two-hundred feet high. They rise abruptly from the plain and are covered with a mixture of native forest and prairie. The loess hill bluffs found in Holt county represent the southernmost extension of the larger formation that extends north along the east side of the Missouri River and into southern South Dakota. These natural features are not only beautiful, but unique to the region with respect to their geology and botany. Some of the plants that grow here are characteristic of the short-grass prairies to the west and are found nowhere else in the state. Excavations or natural washes occasionally have revealed the bones of ancient Pleistocene mammals. Local farmers have found concentrations of Native American artifacts on what apparently were campsites located atop the bluffs. Because of the steepness of the terrain, the bluff faces were not amenable to agriculture and thus largely retained their natural flora. However, a few orchards flourished on the west and south faces of the bluffs until well into the twentieth century, and two towns were built along or on some of the more gentle bluffs: Mound City and Forest City.

Beyond the bluffs to the east and north there is a transition to "rolling" hill country of deep soil intersected frequently by streams and occasionally by severely eroded ditches. The farther from the river the more gentle the terrain. This hill country was cleared of most of the tall-grass and mixed-grass prairie and woodlands after settlement in the 1800s and converted into mixed farms growing corn, oats, hay, some wheat, and livestock—mostly pigs and cattle. Soybeans did not become common until the 1960s.

The deep rich soil, although often abused, supported intensive agriculture. In the 1940s and 1950s, there were as many as four or five farms on each section of land. These farms supported a fairly dense population of relatively prosperous farmers. Although the average farm size probably was about 160 acres, some families made comfortable "livings" from only eighty. One of my neighboring families had only forty acres yet had a good car, a TV, a solid and attractive home, plenty of food grown in a large garden, and adequate goods and medical care. A few houses were occupied by tenant farmers and in some cases two adjacent houses served as homes for members of extended families.

Most of the roads in Holt County are laid out on a strict square mile basis. Originally, out in the country, a single one-room school served families located on the surrounding four sections of land, but well before I entered school the first round of consolidation had occurred (in 1913). In my area children living up to three miles away attended the consolidated school at Bellevue. This school served approximately sixteen to twenty sections of land and in the 1940s provided all twelve grades for approximately ninety students. Bellevue was located out in the country, but each of the other major schools was located in the scattered towns. A few one-room grade schools survived until the early 1950s.

Rural churches were common and relatively conveniently located. Likely they were located according to a particular congregation's needs and with little regard to density. Within the Bellevue school district there were four: Minnesota Valley

Methodist, Pleasant View Presbyterian, Church of the Brethren, and New Liberty Baptist. At the time I write this only New Liberty survives with a small congregation.

In the 1940s, the largest town, Mound City, and many of the smaller towns (Craig, Maitland, Oregon, Forest City), each with populations of five-hundred to slightly over one-thousand, were bustling business centers. Mound City had three clothing stores (Wilsons Men's Shop, Golden Rule, Percy's), two drug stores (Miller's Rexall and Robbin's), three grocery stores, two hardware stores, two barbershops, at least three good cafes, two nursery shops (one of them, Dewey Johns, a fruit store), a large furniture store (Pettijohn and Crawford), a variety store, one MD (Dr. Perry), one DO (Dr. Paul) and notably a movie theater (The State). Also there was a busy creamery that bought eggs and cream from the local farmers and sold livestock feed. On Saturday afternoons the streets were full of folks doing their weekly shopping and visiting, and kids going to the movies and spending their nickels and dimes for sodas and comic books at Miller's drug store.

The rich land and the current economic situation supported a viable, stable and socially thriving agriculture-based economy. As a result there was a strong, stable society centered around school, church and the towns. By today's standards the area served by the local rural schools was small, but in the 1940s the roads were relatively poor. Many were simply graded dirt surfaces. These, and the few gravel-covered roads, often became nearly "bottomless" during the spring thaw and washed out after heavy rain. Consequently the high density of small farms combined with the frequent difficulties of transportation contributed toward centralizing those close-knit communities.

Although this story starts in Nodaway County, a few miles north of Holt County, most of it occurred in the Bellevue community located about five miles northwest of Mound City. This setting was somewhat unusual in that community life was centered around a grade and high school located out in the country rather than in a town.

# THE BEGINNING

I AM TOLD that my entry into this world on a rainy November 1938 night was assisted by a local country doctor who traveled to and from my new home by horse and buggy. He had a considerable distance to come as my first domicile was located about five miles out of town—three miles west and two miles south of Skidmore, Missouri. Skidmore would become newsworthy in the 1980s for events recorded in the book and movie titled *In Broad Daylight*—a true story of 20th century vigilantes dealing with a country bully.

My earliest memories of my first home, the Brown Place, so called because of the owner, not the color of the house, are both fragmented and dim. The small wood-frame house, which faced the county road to the west, was located on a small rise above the dirt road. It had a drive way on the south and a porch to the east. Blue morning glories grew on the fence across the driveway, "Bluwas" as I called them. Dad drove a grey Plymouth car with which he ran over my white kitten in the driveway.

Apparently I barely survived early childhood. I repeatedly "ran off" into the adjoining fields several times with my dog "Goona-goon" (The dog's tail poking above the hay in the fields served as a beacon of my whereabouts), chewed the top off the louse powder container, (lousy chickens, not people), fell on a pair of scissors leaving a scar on my head, and devoured a mushroom (obviously the non-poisonous kind). Otherwise, I had a normal early childhood. My final memory of this home is of my Uncle Raymond helping me load my black and white hobby-horse into the back of a truck in preparation for a move from the Brown Place to the Strough Place.

My father was then a tenant farmer. The Brown Place was only a mile or two from where he grew up. I suspect this first home was selected for proximity to my paternal grandparents. I do not know the details of Dad's agreement with my grandfather, but probably the 1941 move represented Dad's move to independence. It likely was an excellent opportunity for him. The Strough farm was 160 acres of moderately rolling farm land owned by a Mr. D. Strough, an absentee land owner. Not only was the land itself of good quality, but the buildings on the farm were numerous and in excellent condition.

The buildings sat atop a hill located about seven miles northwest of Mound City on the west side of what is now state route C. This location provided beautiful views in all directions. The lovely two-story white house sat near the driveway and next to the road. The wrought iron fence that edged the front of the lawn and the two pillars on the front of the house gave it a relatively elegant appearance. Although the house seemed large to me I think it had only five rooms plus a pantry, but that may be incorrect. To the north along the road there was a row of northern white pine trees and large silver maple trees edged the driveway to the south. A fairly substantial orchard populated with peach and apples trees also was located to the north.

The barns and service buildings, over a dozen of them, were located west and north of the house. The most imposing was the large white horse barn that sat to the southwest at the bottom of a depression. "Down the hill" as we called it. Most of the other buildings were painted barn red. Only the machine storage shed and a couple of corn cribs were unpainted. Today few farmers could afford to build this many buildings—in fact, few could afford to maintain them. (I wonder whether farmers have made any real economic gains since the 1940s.)

Each building had an assigned and separate function. Since

this was a mixed general farm each species had its own barn, i.e., pig, cow, horse and chicken. Consequently each was designed according to that function. The horse barn had individual stalls for each horse, although they usually were paired, a grain bin, and a hay storage area called a mow, (pronounced "maow"). The cow barn had large loafing areas adjacent to a hay mow. The feed racks were located along the sides of the hay mow so the hay could be pitched easily into the racks. The pig building was designed with small pens that each housed a single farrowing sow and her litter. A hallway along one side facilitated access by the farmer, and tip-up doors at the back opened to facilitate removal of the manure.

The wash-smoke house served exactly those functions: to do the laundry and to store the "smoked" meat. Actually in those days the meat was not smoked. Dad bought Morton's smoke salt: a mixture of salt-peter, salt, and brown sugar. This mixture was used to preserve ("cure") the hams, shoulders, and bacon. It was liberally rubbed onto the raw pork. On the hams the mixture was worked in around the shank bone. A thumb hole was punched into the butt end and filled with the mixture. The meat then was laid on a bench, often in a screened box (to keep out the mice) and allowed to cure for several weeks. Then it was hung from cross-rafters in the smoke house. As it hung it dried and absorbed the salt while becoming "country cured." When it came time to eat the ham Mom had to soak the cut slices in water to remove the excess salt.

Even then it was very salty and dry tasting. Nonetheless, hams cured in a similar manner today command top price and are much better tasting than the water-logged variety offered at most super markets.

My memories of life on the Strough Place are a temporal collage—so much so that I find it impossible to write them in chronological order. Those were the years of bonding to parents, assorted dogs, the first pony, extended "explores" to a full five-hundred or so yards from the house, pestering and loving cats, and starting school. Most experiences likely were similar to those of other children growing up on Midwest farms during the 1940s: caring for chicks, calves, colts, and numerous cats; dogs (Gonna goon, Mike, Rover); the dogs catching ground hogs (woodchucks) under the corn crib; (Mike, the rat terrier, would go down the den, and chase the ground hog out of the hole. Rover, the big dog, would grab one end of the poor hog then Mike would come up and grab the other end, and together they would administer the final treatment); and dealing with the occasional skunk in the yard or chicken house. However, three things are especially noteworthy.

The first is that I grew up during the transition on farms from horse to tractor power. In the early 1940s all farmers in that part of the country still relied on horses or mules as their primary source of power for farming. Like others we had several (four) large work horses of the Percheron or Belgium breed to pull the plows and other farm equipment. The horses were of various colors and personalities, but all were large, gentle creatures. Some were geldings and some were mares. Because of their importance they were treated well, and at the Strough Place even had their own barn. Each had a name, such as Blue or Mollie. Although, I do not remember ours by name, I do remember working with them. By six years of age I was allowed to drive a one-row cultivator called a "go-devil" behind them, but because of the perceived danger was not allowed to use the two-row cultivator, mower, or rake. Although planting and cultivation of the row crops was an essential part of the farm year, the most interesting to me was the harvesting: haying, threshing, and shucking.

The hay, usually red clover or alfalfa, was cut with a mower pulled by a team of horses. The turning of the mower wheel was transformed by the gear box on the mower into the power and motion needed to operate the reciprocating cutters. Mowing was a relatively slow process, but rather enjoyable, in that the operator was able to see and smell the hay and watch the occasional rabbit, snake or bird fleeing the mower.

One or two days after mowing, the hay was dry enough to be gathered and consolidated by a dump rake. These machines, pulled by two horses, were about ten to twelve feet long and consisted of a set of long rake tines suspended between two large four or five feet diameter wheels. A seat was mounted above this arrangement so that the driver could control the operations. The operation consisted of driving the length of the field with the tines dropped such that the hay was pulled forward until capacity was reached. The tines then were lifted by actuating gears attached to the wheels. This left a row of piled hay eight to ten feet long. This process was repeated across the field. The driver then turned and came back and dropped another short row beside the first. This operation was repeated until the entire field had been covered. A skilled operator would leave several parallel piles running across the width of the field.

The hay then was either stacked in the field or transferred onto wagons and taken to the barn. The next gathering step usually required a "buck-rake." This machine was constructed of several long narrow pointed poles mounted on a frame that actually was pushed in front of the horses (something like a giant "fork"). By driving the length of a row of raked hay, one could gather it into larger rounded piles. These then were either pushed directly to a stacking site or transferred by two men using pitch forks onto the hay racks (wagons with a large open bed) and then transported to the stack site or to the barns for final storage.

Stacking hay was a hard job requiring several people: those who gathered the hay and brought it to the stack site, and those who piled the hay into the stack. All operations with the dried hay were dusty jobs, especially with red clover hay which had a lot of little hairs on the leaves. Piling was the "skilled" job in that it required keeping the hay piled evenly so that it would stay in place until removed for feeding in the winter. In my part of the country the stacks often were forty or fifty feet long and twenty feet wide by twelve to fifteen feet high. The height often was limited by how high the pitchers could throw the hay from the wagon. However, in some cases stationary mechanical "stackers" were used to raise the hay to the top of the stack. Usually the stacks were capped with sheets of tar paper, over which more hay was piled and then old tires or other heavy items used to hold that in place. A good stack could last two years, but in most cases they were used during the winter following their construction.

Threshing was a major event for each farm and a community activity. Few farmers owned their own threshing machines. Instead the owner of the machine moved from farm to farm and members of the community helped each other with the threshing. We still used stationary threshing machines powered by a stationary tractor—we had passed out of the steam engine era. Although both wheat and oats were harvested in this manner, oats, because it was good horse feed, was our main crop.

The process began when the grain reached the appropriate stage of ripeness—usually tested by rubbing a few grains out of the head and biting them. A reaper, also called a binder, pulled by either two or four horses, was used to cut the standing grain. The binder was a fancy mowing machine that bundled the stalks with heads of grain attached, wrapped each bundle with a string (binder twine) and dropped the bundle on the ground. (It should be noted that the McCormick Reaper was a major advance in agricultural mechanization.) The bundles then were manually stacked into "shocks" standing upright to facilitate the drying of the grain. The shocks stood in the field until the threshing machine arrived and was placed at a chosen location in the field. Two or more men, using pitch forks, tossed the shocked grain onto hay racks and transported it to the receiving end of the threshing machine. There it was pitched into the machine which separated straw from grain. The grain then came spewing out of a spout into a waiting wagon while the straw came out the far end of the machine.

The actual threshing was the highlight of the operation. I distinctly remember the giant noisy machine, the long slapping belt from the tractor to the pulley on the machine, the grain and straw spewing into the wagon and onto the ground, the shouts of the workers, the horses and wagons pulled among the other machinery, and the distinctive sweet smell of the grain. This whole operation was silhouetted against the green of the trees at the edge of the field and the blue of the summer sky.

The operation did not end with threshing. The grain then had to be transported to the barn and scooped shovel-full by shovel-full into the grain bin. The straw usually was either stacked or pitched onto hay racks and transported to the hay mow for storage as bedding for the animals to lie on during the winter. In the mid-40s it often was pitched into a stationary hay bailer and the big square bales were taken to the barn.

One notable thing about both haying and threshing is that they tended to be operations in which members of the community went from farm to farm to help each other. In fact haying remained that way well into the 1950s. Apparently the various involved farmers negotiated the order of doing each others' crops based on maturity of the crops and perhaps acreage. Along with the communal work went communal eating. The household of the place at which the harvest was occurring hosted the workers, although in some cases the neighboring wives also came along to help cook. The output of the cooks and the input of the workers usually was relatively huge. Midday meals (called dinner in the country) always consisted of meat, potatoes, other in-season vegetables, usually pies and lots of iced tea or lemonade. I suspect some tables were favored over others, and I recall one lady who was unappreciated because she wrapped the legs of her dining table with news papers so the men would not scratch it with their work boots. Without a doubt though the communal work contributed very positively to joy of life and likely made the heavy work seem much lighter.

It was while we were threshing that the second important event occurred at the Strough place. I do not know whether someone came to the field to tell Dad or whether he found out directly, but apparently it was the former manner in which he first found out that Mom was ill. In any case the illness was diagnosed as undulant fever, or brucellosis, caught from drinking milk from one of my grandfather Loucks' apparently untested cows. This occurred probably in 1942 or 1943 and before penicillin was available. Consequently Mom had about four very difficult years in and out of remission and in and out of the hospital until she finally became mobile again. She suffered the residual effects for years afterwards. As a result of her illness I became relatively independent from the age of four or five through age seven. Dad was busy in the field and Mom was incapacitated so I had relatively little supervision. I learned to entertain myself and developed independence—a trait that I carried into later life. Also I learned rudimentary cooking such as boiling potatoes and frying meat, although I was limited in this endeavor by the difficulty of operating a kerosene-fired cook stove.

Our tenure at the Strough place was ended by a third major event, a tornado. It struck on a hot June afternoon in 1946. I was in the garden south of the house picking strawberries into an aluminum cooking pan. I looked up and saw a giant dark cloud at the Horton house about one-half mile to the south, southwest. I also saw a large chunk of their barn roof go flying out from the cloud. I ran across the garden and driveway into the house to tell Dad, "Horton's house is on fire." Memories of the next few minutes are blurred as I was rushed into the storm cellar located west of the house with Dad, Mom, the hired man, and a neighbor, Landon Seitz, who drove into the driveway, parked his car and rushed to the cellar with us. The men closed the upper door,then stood at the lower door holding it shut while we listened to a tremendous roar and bangs and ripping sounds coming from above. That lasted only two or three minutes, then it was quiet.

When we emerged all had been changed. Some of the bricks had been blown out of the structure of the cellar entry arch. The big white horse barn had been turned upside down—the horses had escaped unharmed. The other barns were gone. The granary had been moved off its foundation. The house had been shoved aside and most of the windows blown out. A large roll of woven wire sat in the corner of the now filthy kitchen. The garage was gone and Dad's car, which had been in the garage, had been carried about two-hundred feet and wrapped around the trunk of a de-topped pine tree. The neighbor's car, which had been parked beside the garage, was still there with only a small crack in one window. The lots and yard were full of debris.

The tornado had hit in late afternoon and soon it was dark. I was bundled up and sent off to my grandmother Loucks' house along with Mom. I do not know how long we stayed there, but when I returned the damage was even more evident and crowds of people were walking among the wreckage.

Two incidents illustrate both the power and long-term effects of the wind. The first happened several weeks later after some of the fences had been repaired. I was out in the lots, and started to climb over one of the board fences. Part way over I felt a pain in my leg. On investigating I found a deep cut about an inch long. The source proved to be a piece of glass that had been driven completely through a one-inch thick cypress fence board. I still carry that scar.

The second resulted directly from the storm, but its full effects occurred only several years later. My dog, Rover, a beautiful white Shepard cross-breed, apparently had crawled under the granary to escape the storm. As a result of the storm damage he was trapped under the remains of that building. We found him the next day with his nose sticking through a crack in the boards. We soon freed him. Although perfectly mobile he had a large and noticeable bruise on his head that went untreated. He seemed to recover physically and remained a good hunter, but never was "quite right" after that. The once friendly dog became very shy and was particularly fearful of strangers. He stayed around our three subsequent homes for the next two or three years, but began running with a pack of dogs. He met his demise when a neighbor caught them chasing pigs. The neighbor let the dogs follow the pigs in the hog house, shut the door on them, and as they emerged one by one sent them to dog heaven.

The biggest impact of the tornado was the loss of our house and most of the farm buildings. Dad rigged temporary and makeshift quarters for the livestock, but we had no choice but to look for another place to live. He kept the crops and farmed the acreage that summer, but eventually most of the remaining buildings, with the exception of a corn crib and the hog house, were torn down and burned. Some of the lots were converted to fields. Today there is little remaining of that once beautiful farm complex: a few weathered outbuildings and a cattle feed lot.

In retrospect, I wonder how my parents, particularly Dad, withstood two major setbacks in such a short time: first Mom catching a very serious illness and then the tornado. Many would have been broken, but they were made of strong stuff. Fortunately they also had the support of my grandparents and some very fine neighbors.

# THE TRANSITION

AFTER THE TORNADO we found temporary quarters about one and one-half miles north of the Strough Place in a house which I believe was owned the county assessor. It was a rather small two-story structure, poorly painted, apparently vacant for some time, and accompanied by an unpainted garage and chicken house that was surrounded by abandoned farm equipment. There was a water-well topped with the usual iron hand pump and a storm cellar with sloped wooden doors that opened directly above the steps. We lived only in the first floor of the house because a previous occupant had raised baby chicks upstairs where newspapers, covered with droppings, carpeted the floor. Fortunately there was an outside entrance to the upstairs, thus the odor did not penetrate to the downstairs.

Dad drove back and forth to the Strough Place to do the farming while Mom and I usually stayed around the house. We had neither livestock nor garden at this house, thus there was not a lot for me to do. However, I did manage to occupy myself. Among other things I stirred up a nest of bumble bees and got severely stung, ate mulberries that grew behind the deserted chicken house, and with a friend who lived nearby learned to smoke cigarette stubs at the age of seven. I also occasionally wandered down to the Strough place to poke around the ruins. But that activity was curtailed by a very frightening event—one that affected me for a long time.

Dad, for fear of my being injured, did not want me playing around the damaged buildings. One day curiosity got the best of me and I was peeking into or actually had gone into the still standing windowless farm house. As I entered I heard a thud and a loud growl. I cleared out immediately, ran out of the house, across the driveway and down into the lots—apparently clearing a fairly high fence in the process. I learned later that day that the thud was caused by a piece of dirt thrown into the building and that the growl was made by Dad. Still, I was so scared by that event that I had nightmares that night and was afraid of the dark for a couple of years thereafter. If Dad had suspected that his approach would have had that effect he likely would have used a different one, but I stayed out of the old house after that.

For reasons that we never knew, before the summer was over the house owner allegedly had the sheriff serve Dad an eviction notice even though the rent was paid. In any case, we had to move again. From there we went a couple of miles west to a place almost as bad: a huge old empty structure known to us as the Long house. Although this house was very large, with eight or nine rooms, we occupied only three or four on the ground floor. My parents must have been near exhaustion from cleaning up messes that year—particularly since Mom was not well to begin with. The Long house was located at least three miles from the Strough Place, thus Dad had a greater distance to go to do the farming. Because he still had animals, that trip had to be made every day regardless of the weather. Today three miles is a tiny distance over reasonable roads, but in those days most of the roads were still dirt surfaced and in wet weather often nearly impassable.

In one respect the location of the Long house was fortuitous in that it gave me a brief experience in a one-room country school. Lonesome School was located on the northwest corner of the section and about one quarter mile north of the Long house. It was the typical square wood frame structure with white paint, a single door opening to the south and one large room with windows on the west. A shed for horses was located down the hill to the south and beyond that the privies. A well and pump located outside provided water. A single, large potbellied stove, located in the southwest corner, provided the heat.

I entered the third grade that fall of 1946 under the care of Miss Hutton—a pretty blond young teacher. There were only about a dozen students of all ages in grades one through eight. I later attended high school with Don Salfrank and Gene Miller, but the names of most of the others are lost from memory. Some moved out of the community and others went to a different high school. I also remember the biggest boy, Toby, who rode a horse to school. He was somewhat of a bully and I caught some of his ire. I was accused of tripping some traps which another student had set in an attempt to catch a ground hog that had a den across the road from the school. I do not remember the details, but I do know I was "picked on" after that. It probably was more a case of being the new kid than anything else. On the other hand I became a regular playmate of Don and his younger brother Byron, and remained friends with Don through college.

In some ways I was lucky to have had this brief experience. I retain pleasant memories of those few months—particularly of the big old stove. Not only was it a source of warmth, but when we studied "Indians" we made pots from the clay dug from banks across the road and then baked them on the stove.

We also had school performances. I was there for the Halloween party and play. The stage was one empty corner of the room. Across this was a curtain made of burlap and supported by a piece of wire tacked to the adjoining walls. Simple, but it served the purpose. The details of the program are forgotten, but the main song was titled *Sioux City Sue*—a popular western song of the time. The words contained the phrase: "Sioux City Sue, hair of gold, eyes of blue, I would swap my horse and dog for you, goin to take you with my old lasso."

My stay at Lonesome ended in November,1946, when we moved yet again to a farm Dad had bought and I then transferred back to the reorganized Bellevue School. Lonesome School closed within a few years. My parents remained at the new farm, the Home Place, for over forty years. My brother Paul was born here in 1948. Dad passed away in 1985 and lies in the New Liberty Cemetery overlooking the farm. Mom lived there until about 1997 and still owns the farm land. In a very real sense this is where the story of *"Going After The Cows"* really starts.

# THE HOME PLACE

MY PARENTS CLEARLY were people of great courage and resilience. Looking back I am amazed that they made the recovery from the tornado's devastation of their rented farm to the purchase of a fairly run down, but promising, farm in fewer than six months. The new farm, previously owned by a Mr. Buetzer, once had been a show place with a lake and race track located on the flat areas south of the farmstead. However, over time many of the buildings, though still solid, had weathered and deteriorated. Shortly after we moved into the new place, Dad hired a carpenter (Mr. Jess Bullock) who stayed with us and worked full-time for several months. Mr. Bullock made extensive repairs to the barns, put new porches on the house, built new lot fences, and eventually tore down the dilapidated garage and replaced it with a garage-machine shed combination. The fact that Dad could afford this level of help, apparently starting with relatively little capital, speaks loudly about the farm economy in those days and about Dad's ability as a manager and his capacity for hard work. Apparently all of the building and repairing went well––except for the garage-machine shop. Not to do anything half-way they designed it as a three-bay building constructed of pole supports and sided with tongue and groove pine lumber (probably unaffordable today). All went well until the rafters were put up before the tie beams were put in place (It was whispered that the carpenter had nipped too much cheap wine, which he apparently kept hidden in the barn). As a result the roof bowed.

Although efforts were made to eliminate the bow, they were only partially successful, and to this day the roof sags in the middle.

The farmland was not in very good condition. Uncontrolled erosion had resulted in several very deep ditches. Over the years these were filled and dammed. The soil was restored by careful crop rotation. The fields were fenced with literally miles of barbed wire and woven wire fence. These fences, while controlling the animals, also served effectively in some cases as *de facto* terraces to reduce run-off and provide cover for wildlife. Gradually the farm was restored to one with well-kept red barns, white house and out-buildings, fenced fields and mowed fence rows.

The farm is located three miles north of the bluffs that mark the north edge of the Missouri River valley as it swings to the west. Like the surrounding area it is largely a moderately rolling terrain of hills intersected by partially wooded streams. Our one-hundred twenty acres is located in the southwest corner of the section bordered by what now is Ironwood Road and 140. The southwest corner of the farm is largely flat stream-bottom land of very rich Marshall silt loam. When we first moved there, about ten acres of this was undrained marsh. This flat area gradually joins the hills to the east and north. Bisecting the hills are two small streams. Both are wooded, and at that time one was at least fifteen feet deep. One of Dad's first projects was to dam this stream in three places to create three ponds which became attractive to migrating ducks, and, unknown to my parents, swimming holes.

The surrounding country-side is of the same general terrain. The result is a very "warm secure" country with the farmsteads either sheltered in the valley or placed on the hill tops. Those on the hill tops, though exposed, have superb views across the rolling countryside. The ridge located one-half mile east of our house forms a divide. To the east water runs directly to Squaw Creek. To the west it runs into Wildcat Creek (labeled West Branch in the 1918 Atlas) which then joins Squaw Creek about two and one-half miles to the south. From the top of that divide one can see two miles west, four miles north or east, and ten to fifteen miles south across the Missouri River valley into Kansas and Nebraska. The view to and above the next ridge to the west is particularly beautiful at sunset. West of that ridge the drainage flows into the Little Tarkio Creek and immediately into the Missouri River valley. In the days of my boyhood great flights of ducks and geese, as they returned down the river valleys to the game refuge, often were silhouetted against the red, orange and pink autumn sunsets.

Dad was a general farmer growing corn, oats, wheat, pigs, cows, chickens and hay. Thus, the fields were small (ten-forty acres) and diversified. In addition to various crops we had a variety of weeds, a few wild flowers, lots of birds and some interesting mammals. Wildcat Creek located just across the road west of the house supported a good population of bullheads, carp and various small sunfish. In the fall the cornfields attracted ducks and geese by the thousands and often we had a few quail and a pair of pheasants. The hayfields supported good populations of birds, woodchucks, and plains pocket gophers (*Geomys bursarius*). The gopher mounds were a nuisance, but we generally tolerated them as a curiosity and occasionally one could see the big brown gophers poke their heads out of the ground as they dug a new tunnel. Sadly they are gone now, no doubt due to pesticide poisoning and the switch to high intensity row crop farming. In the early 1960s a badger (*Taxidea taxis*) appeared in one of our alfalfa fields. His presence was obvious by the large den-opening which was cavernous enough to nearly engulf the front wheels of a tractor. I saw him only once. Apparently the badger family, if there was one, perished because they were never seen after that first year. Although not a biological paradise, this farm was a wonderful place for a budding naturalist to grow up. As a result I formed, and retain, a great affection for this and the surrounding countryside. It is difficult to articulate the "feel for the land" that I developed at this farm; a feeling that grows as the years pass. Indeed I still derive pleasure, joy and satisfaction from just walking over the place.

The white farm house stood (stands) on the east side of the road and on the top of a bank formed by two intersecting streams—Wildcat Creek to the west and an unnamed rivulet to the south. This location provides views past the two barns and over the valley to the south and one partially obstructed by trees to the west. During my childhood a large grove of magnificent American and slippery elm trees stood north and northeast of the house and two pignut hickory trees provided shade in the south part of the lawn. In the 1960s the elms gradually succumbed to Dutch elm disease and one of the hickories to old age.

The house was the classic two story, "T"-shaped, wood-frame house. The base of the T formed the family-dining room. The "living room" was located in the northwest wing of the T and a bedroom the northeast wing of the T. A bathroom was added by my parents in the 1960s. The kitchen, located east of the dining room, had been added after the original house was built, but several years before we moved in. The three upstairs rooms served as bedrooms and a storage ("junk") room. I immediately moved into the south upstairs room which served as my room until I left for college, and usually as the room I and my family slept in on our subsequent visits home. My brother eventually moved into the north room. That remained his room until he went off to college.

The heating system was first one, and later two, oil-fired stoves placed in the dining room and living room downstairs. The first winter we had only one heating stove and I remember setting "ice cream" mix into the northeast room one day to freeze. It did! Usually the downstairs was comfortable during the winter— even if you did have to sit or stand next to the stove to get really warm, but the upstairs always was cold. In winter, my routine for preparing for bed was to warm by the stove then literally run upstairs, quickly remove my clothes and jump into the freezing bed. I do not remember whether I slept in pajamas or underwear as a boy, but I do know I had lots of blankets and covered myself completely. There was an opening called a "register" located in the floor of the south bedroom upstairs. It was positioned just over the stove downstairs. In winter the register was opened to allow heat to rise from the stove below. It was modestly effective, but the south room never became "toasty-warm" and the north bedroom, which lacked a register, always was cold although never below freezing. Never-the-less I always slept well.

In summer the south bedroom was ventilated by opening the south-facing windows and the west- facing door that opened onto the porch roof. Usually there was a good breeze at night. For this I was thankful: we did not have an electric fan during the early years. I eventually partially solved that problem by cutting a fan blade from a piece of thin sheet metal and attaching it to the main drive of the electric motor from my Erector set. The blade was only about eight inches long and without a safety shield, but it gave a good breeze when set on a low table by the window.

We did not have electricity when we first moved into the Home Place, but the house was wired soon after. I do not remember whether the REA already had a line down that road at the time of our move, but shortly after they brought through a three-wire main line. With the arrival of electricity Dad bought Mom a Philco refrigerator and an electric Speed Queen washer. Mom also got a new bottled-gas cook stove and an electric iron. All of these appliances, particularly the refrigerator, represented a major improvement for her. While at the Strough Place and during the transition period after the tornado we still used an ice box which required weekly replenishment with a fifty pound block of ice obtained from the ice company in Mound City.

We did not get running water for several years. Before that all of the water for domestic use was obtained by a hand-operated pump installed in the well near the back door. Drinking water was put into a bucket that sat on a cabinet inside and near the back kitchen door. A communal dipper was used for drinking—a standard and common practice in those days. We did not switch to individual glasses until running water was installed in the kitchen about 1950.

Washing of hands and face was done in a wash pan that sat on that cabinet and waste water was put into a "slop bucket" that was pitched over the fence into the hog lot or chicken yard. In the summer the wash pan sat on a bench outside. We pumped water into the pan, washed, dried on a communal towel, and then tossed the water on the grass. We were not "backward" in this respect. It was the common practice. Actually it was very practical as the men usually got very dirty in the fields and slopped a lot while washing. It kept the water off of the floors and made good use of the wash water. Until the bathroom was installed we used a combination of chamber pot and outdoor privy which, fortunately, was located some distance from the house and downhill from the well. The privy always was smelly and a little dirty—especially in the summer. I became sanitation conscious and covered the seat and floor with light-colored linoleum (it was the brightest privy in the area) and used quicklime to reduce the contents. The "old" Sears and Roebuck catalogs served as a source of paper for many years.

Using the privy in winter required both motivation and stamina. I always waited until the last minute to go and then made the visit as short as possible. It was not a time for contemplation. In retrospect, it really did not hurt us at all. No one froze a finger or behind, or caught a cold, using the privy in winter. Although I am thankful for modern facilities, I also realize how relatively pampered we are today when I see some of the stuff put into modern bathrooms, e.g., fuzzy seat covers.

However, getting a bathroom probably was one of the most enjoyed home improvements for my mother. It served two purposes: abolishment of the privy (which later was torn down and the hole filled) and provision of a private, warm place to take a bath. Before the bathroom we took turns using the living room so that we could stand by the stove to take our sponge bath in the winter. By today's standards it was a bit Spartan, but in retrospect was both adequate and sensible. Today we probably use about ten to twenty gallons of water to take a shower. In those days one or two gallons was adequate. It still is, we are just very wasteful. Bathing in the summer was less of a problem for the men of the house. We could take the wash-tub behind the cellar, out of sight of the house, and take a real bath using "lots" of water. There was no problem if it splashed on the grass as the waste was used to water the grass or garden.

Mom never got an automatic washer while on the farm. The water supply likely was inadequate, and the plumbing system surely was. Instead she used the electric ringer washer. The wash water was heated on the stove in big boilers and then dumped into the washer. Rinse water was put cold into two large tubs sitting side by side. The sequence was wash, run the clothes through the wringer to save the wash water, rinse in the first tub, wring and run into the second tub, wring again and then hang the clothes on the outdoor line to dry. White dainties were washed first, then the less dainty underwear and socks and finally the grubby work clothes. In that way the entire wash could be done with three existing tubs of water. This was a very good way of conserving water, although I suppose the wash water was changed if it got too bad. All of that water had to be pumped by hand. One dry summer the well at the house nearly dried up. As a result I carried water about one-hundred yards from the wells at the barns, thus there was good reason to conserve it. In any case the process was quite effective. Whites were white, and helped to stay that way by rinsing in a "bluing" solution—a practice not used in today's automatic washers.

America must be one of the few countries in which most wash-ladies no longer use clothes lines(as we learned on our sabbatical leave in England). The attractiveness of the electric dryer to modern folk is understandable, but they miss a lot by not hanging clothes on a line. A pair of stiffly frozen long-johns or blue jeans is much more interesting than a crumpled hot heap taken from the dryer. With the dryer there is no reason to look outside to see if the rain clouds are moving your way, or to notice whether the robins are eating cherries. The smell of the hot bundle from the dryer can hardly compare with the cool-crisp freshness of a load from the line, particularly in winter. The beauty and joy of line-drying have a price, but those joys of being outside and being aware of what is going on there probably are worth it. There is something elemental about hanging clothes out to dry and artistically beautiful about towels, sheets and skirts blowing in the wind. Maybe it is the thought that nature's breezes and sunlight are making the very clothes we wear wearable—a special reminder of the relationship between man and the fundamental elements of nature.

I find it interesting that the hanging of clothes was affected by changes in technology. Even clothes pins and clothes line wire changed with time. The older clothes pins were stiff straight wood devices that clamped the clothing into a slot pushed over the line. Then came the modern version: wooden squeeze style with wire springs to hold them shut, and even these were replaced with plastic. Likewise the original nine-gauge galvanized wire was replaced with plastic coated aluminum. All were considerable improvements.

I grew up during the time of transition from stove-heated irons to electric irons. I do not remember the event of Mom getting her General Electric iron, but I am sure it was a joy and great time-saver for her. She usually ironed in the dining room— probably because we kept the radio, TV, and heating stove in that room. Although she did most of the ironing, I did learn how to iron while still in grade school. It came in handy later, and I am glad to say that I still know how to iron a shirt or pair of pants although I do not get much pleasure from the practice.

THE HOUSE AT THE HOME PLACE
( circa 1990)

THE HOUSE AND BIG BARN
Note the elm trees in the background  (circa 1960)

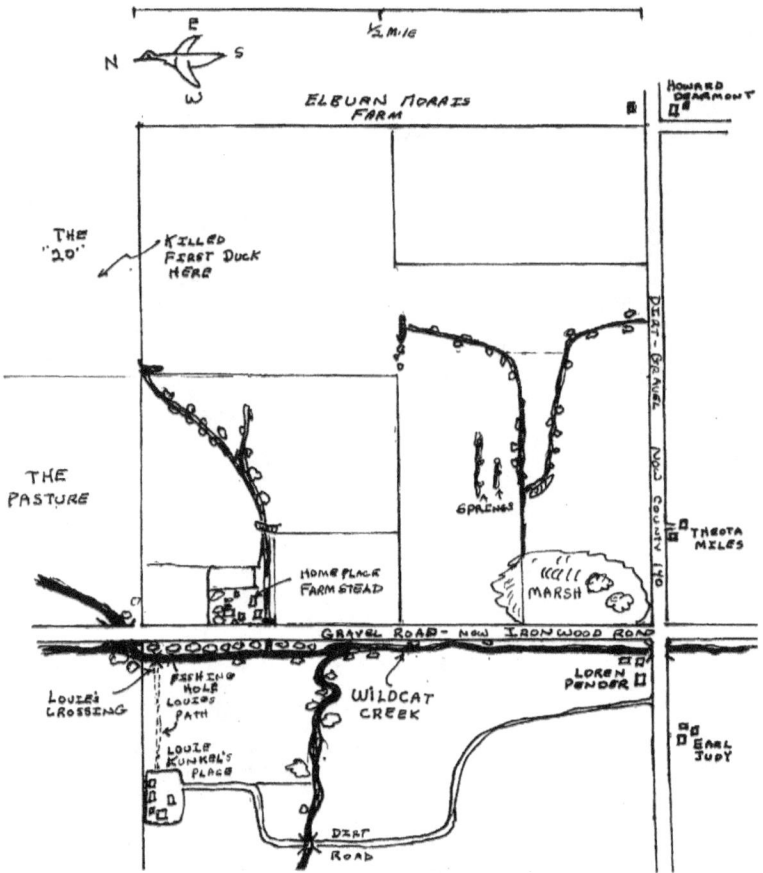

THE HOME PLACE AND LOCATION OF SOME ADJACENT NEIGHBORS
AS OF ABOUT 1950

# THE BARNS

ALTHOUGH MY PARENTS gave due attention to repairing and improving the house, equal attention was given to the animal quarters—which in some ways were considered the really important buildings on the farm. We had several small outbuildings, but only two true barns. All were kept in good condition and the barns, being painted barn-red and trimmed with white, were truly beautiful. The larger one had a striking green roof topped with two lighting rods on which rotated small and intricate weather vanes. In comparison modern steel buildings are largely lacking in aesthetic appeal—a Major loss for this country. The larger barn served multiple functions: equipment storage, grain storage(three bins), hay storage(up in the mow), and animal shelter. An alley-way, or hall, ran the length of the center. The grain bins were located along the north side and the feed bunks for the horses and cows were on the south side. The barn was designed to hold six horses in three double stalls. Each stall had two grain boxes, one located on either side of the central hay bunk that ran along the front of the stall. The grain bins were about six inches deep by twelve by twenty inches square. The central hay bunks measured about six to eight feet long by two to three feet deep. We gave the horses oats or whole ears of corn which they ate by effectively shelling the grain off the cobs. Horses were good suppliers of cobs—which earlier families took to the house and used to start the wood or coal fires in the cook or heating stoves. Cobs also served as a form of emergency barn-toilet paper for some farmers. The horses also were fed plenty of hay. Their favorite was timothy or a mixture of timothy and red clover. We also used the big barn as a milking parlor for our one or two milk cows in the winter and after all of the horses had been sold one stall was converted for use in the spring as a farrowing pen for two sows.

The big barn was a community to itself that served as a retreat for both the animals and me. Among the animal occupants were several cats who slept and raised their kittens there. When we were milking they sat attentively, eagerly awaiting their share of the fresh milk. Semi-wild bantam chickens perched on the rafters or edge of the hay bunks and often nested under the bunks. Thus, they usually were present in both the early morning and evening. In addition to the adult animals, there were at times calves, piglets, chicks and kittens to feed, pet, or just admire. Nature also provided barn swallows which typically had two or three nests plastered onto the six by six oak ceiling joists. Of course English sparrows were about, and always there were a few pigeons nesting in the hay mow.

This mixed set of animal companions provided a unique background of memorable, soothing sounds. I enjoyed most the "crunch-crunch" of the horses chewing, the occasional "nicker" and the periodic stomping of their feet. Aside from an occasional "moo" the cows did not make much noise as they ate the chopped pieces of corn whole and consumed their hay relatively delicately. The cats mewed softly from their various locations on the floor or the edges of the hay bunks. The chickens were quiet except for periodic cackle, although early in the morning the roosters would crow loudly until displaced from their perches. I always knew the pigeons were present by their cooing and the noisy flap of their wings as they flew in and out of the barn. In summer the barn swallows provided their very soft chirps and cheeps as they came and went about feeding their young or sat outside and rested between their flights to catch bugs. All of this life occurred in one small barn—an enclosed space of only about forty by forty feet. The animals provided excellent company.

Sadly, the sounds of the "big barn" no longer exist for most American farm kids. With the exception of Amish communities, and a few kept as pets, work horses are no longer found on American farms. Pigs are now raised in confinement buildings built over manure storage pits. The concentrations of ammonia in the air often is staggering and there is little aesthetic appeal in the steel and concrete walkways. Feed delivery often is controlled by a computer. Cows are housed in concrete-floored loafing barns (admittedly an improvement over dirt floors), but instead of the "scuzz-scuzz" of the hand delivered milk hitting the other milk in the bucket, one hears the "slug-slug" or whine of the milking machine. Barn swallows still frequent the oft abandoned barns, but there is no one around to see or hear them. A few cats may prowl and share the barn with the wildlife, but unless they live on a dairy farm their food likely comes from the supermarket because relatively few farmers now bother to keep a milk cow.

Although our "little" barn also had multiple functions it served primarily as a combination corn crib and loafing shed for the cows and pigs. There was a corn crib on either side of the drive through alley-way. The ears of corn, and later the shelled corn, were brought from the field and stored here for the winter. Small doors at one end allowed for removal of the grain as needed. It was fed to both cows and pigs. For the pigs it usually was scooped directly onto the ground or into troughs near the barn.

There was an open three sided "lean-too" shed attached to the south side of this barn. It served primarily as a loafing shed for the beef cows and pigs during the winter, although it could double for hay storage. Since this building was primarily for storage and shelter I spent little time there. However, one special event sometimes occurred late in the summers when the corn was nearly used up from the cribs and only a small pile left in one end. All of the barns were well populated with mice and an occasional rat, but they congregated in large numbers in the corn cribs. When the eared corn was nearly gone it was easy to move about, so I would take one or two of my favorite cats into the crib, shut the door behind us, and scoop the corn about to flush the mice. The cats were in cat heaven!!! Usually I would flush several mice at once—sometimes more than the cats could handle. Often the cats tried to carry one mouse in their mouth while pursuing another. In any case they got well fed while exercising their hunting abilities and performing a service for us.

My father raised over one-hundred pigs each year, but he never had a really proper "hog-house." Instead he used smaller movable sheds in which to farrow the sows and let the growing pigs use the barns or a larger shed for loafing and sleeping once they had been weaned. The smaller sheds were portable and for several years he moved them out to one of the hay fields for farrowing the sows. This practice likely reduced disease because the animals were moved to clean ground. However, during the 50s the farrowing sheds sat in the big lot below the farm house. The smaller sheds were about twenty feet long and perhaps ten feet wide. Each was divided into two ten by ten foot pens into which was placed one sow for farrowing and early care of her piglets. There were doors into each pen on the front of the house and a door on the roof of each pen. The roof door served two purposes: to expedite cleaning and on warm sunny days they could be opened to allow the sow and piglets to bask in the late winter or spring sun. We had four or five of those small sheds. In addition sows were farrowed in two pens built into the south side of the big barn and in a pen in the small barn. The sheds and barn were unheated, but we solved that problem by running electrical cords to the shed and hanging heat lamps from the ceiling. In the barn we also hung heat lamps, but from sockets that had been wired into the pens. By today's standards this seems a relatively primitive approach, but the use of heat lamps was considered a significant advance for warming the piglets and reducing piglet mortality.

The small sheds were efficient for the intended job, but their size resulted in one of the worst jobs on the farm: cleaning them.

Although pigs are fairly fastidious animals that tend to drop their manure in one corner rather than at random, the straw and manure had to be removed and replaced with clean bedding on a regular basis. These sheds were so low that even I could not stand up and always was bumping my head or back. The only consolation was watching the piglets and the joy of finishing the job!

Like most other farmers of that era we had a chicken house and raised chickens for meat and eggs. Ours was fairly nice: about 450 square feet with a sloping roof high enough to allow humans to stand upright. It had windows and two doors: one as the entry-way and the other to the chicken-yard located adjacent to the house. The chicken house sheltered the laying hens and the two or three accompanying roosters throughout the year. It served as protection from the weather and predators, provided a loafing-feeding area, and more importantly for us a place for the hens to lay their eggs.

Inside it was divided into three general areas: roost, laying boxes, and loafing-feeding area. The roost was constructed of large one-inch diameter sticks about eight feet long nailed to cross pieces and suspended two or three feet above the straw-covered dirt floor. The chickens perched on it at night when sleeping. In the northwest corner there were two rows of laying boxes, each about twelve-inch cubes open on the front. A three- or four-inch board was attached to the bottom front to keep the contents(straw and eggs) inside. The floor of the cubicles was filled with straw to attract the hens and help keep the eggs intact and clean. In most cases the hens instinctively entered the cubicles to deposit their daily egg. Apparently they just used the cubicles to lay in, because often there were multiple eggs in each cubicle each night when I went "to get the eggs." This meant that multiple hens had used that cubicle that day. However, some hens were fickle and would lay their eggs in the corner of the house on the floor or in some other site. This was a problem when the chosen corner was located under the roost.

The part of the chicken house floor located near the entry door held the feed and water pans and provided a loafing area for the birds. However, in the good weather the birds were let outside either into the whole farmyard or into the "chicken yard." The chicken yard was a fifteen by twenty feet square area fenced with woven wire that attached to the south side of the chicken house. The fence was about eight to ten feet high—so constructed to keep the chickens from flying out. The yard was used as the day-area during much of the year, but particularly during warmer days of winter. At other times the chickens were allowed the run of the farm to search for bugs and whatever else they could find to eat—including the undigested grains of corn that passed through the digestive tracts of the cows. However, most of them found their way back to the "hen-house" at night where they could roost behind closed doors safe from raccoons, foxes and skunks. The bantams on the other hand, were independent little devils that liked to roost in the barns or other out buildings and in some cases in trees.

We did not have a special brooder house in which to keep young chicks until they were old enough to withstand daily temperature changes and know enough to get in out of the rain. Although one or two of our laying hens would sneak off into the weeds in the spring and hatch a brood of chicks, that was not a significant source of either replacement hens or young roosters (cockerels) to be used for the dinner table. Most of our chicks were obtained from a nearby hatchery although some were obtained via the U.S. Postal Service. They were shipped from a hatchery right after hatching, and by virtue of the retained yolk-sac had sufficient stored nutrients to survive a few days if kept warm. Immediately upon receipt they would be put into a brooder facility and supplied with starter feed and water and with a source of heat. They instinctively knew to peck at the feed and to drink the water and survived well if given these requirements. Since we did not have a specific brooder house we substituted one side of one of the portable pig sheds—after cleaning it well. The shed was moved close enough to the farm house to permit a one-hundred foot extension cord to reach it. This provided a source of power for a heat lamp that hung a couple of feet above the floor. The chicks would gather below the lamp and make little sounds of contentment in the warmth.

Losses were few and growth was rapid. After two weeks the chicks' wings had very distinctive feather buds and the down was disappearing. About this time I usually picked out the cockerels with the largest combs as pets. These birds got more attention than the others, although I doubt that they really enjoyed being caught, carried around, and stroked. They did benefit with a longer life-span though as one or more usually graduated each year to the hen-house to serve as "flock masters" until age or predators took them away. The fate of the other youngsters was programmed to be otherwise. Cockerels were eaten, pullets either eaten or a few kept to be egg producers. Mom never kept many layers, so most of the pullets met the same fate as their male companions.

# GOING AFTER THE COWS

SEVERAL PASTURES PROVIDED summer grazing for our small herd of Shorthorn beef cows and one to three milk cows. A small pasture of about five acres led north from the barn lots. A larger one of about thirty acres, called the "big" pasture,was rented from our neighbor Carl Nauman.  It started at the half-section line and extended to the north for one-quarter of a mile.  The "big" pasture was not large by adult standards, but to a growing boy it represented miles of imaginary "jungle" or "plains" inhabited by outlaws, foreign soldiers (I grew up during and shortly after World War II) and wild animals.  Actually the big pasture was mostly a hillside that occupied the northeast slope of a forty-acre field.  From the top of the hill one could see several miles to the north and south and at least one mile to the next ridges to the east and west.  At the bottom of the hill Wildcat Creek bordered the northwest side of the pasture.  The west side of the stream was so steep that neither cow nor man could go up it.  This apparently resulted from a channelization project carried out in the 1930s.  The east bank of this stream was bordered with scattered box elder and silver maple trees—perfect places for cows to loaf in the summer.  Small grassy or tree-lined ditches ran from the east down into the main stream bed.  These provided access to the stream for the cows and "canyons" for me to play in.

Dad usually turned all of the cows into this pasture in early spring and allowed them to largely care for themselves.  The pasture provided plenty of grass and the creek provided water.  The only extra we provided was a salt block and periodic checks on their condition. The beef cows remained undisturbed in the pasture all summer.

However, we also always kept a few dairy or "milk" cows as sources of milk, cream, and butter for our table. The excess cream was sold to a local creamery. Over the years the cows were of various colors and breeding, but usually at least part Guernsey— selected for the fact that their milk was high in butter fat. Blackie was part Guernsey, but endowed with small horns and a mostly black coat. Daisy, my favorite, was a purebred yellow and white Guernsey that Dad drove all the way to Wisconsin to purchase. Daisy had a "sister," but her name is lost—in part because she did not perform well (give much milk) and was sold a year or two after purchase. During the winter the milk cows, like the beef cows, were kept in lots near the barns. But in the summer they were turned out into the big pasture every morning so they could enjoy the company of their beefy comrades during the day. Every evening it was my job to go after the cows (or cow —depending on our ambitions) prior to milking time.

This usually was a pleasant task that provided a small adventure in getting away from the house. At first I accomplished the task on foot, but soon I got a pony. Actually there were in succession three: Brownie, Trigger, Flicka. Finally about the time I entered high school I moved into the mechanical age and often used the tractor. The tractor was especially useful when the cultivator was mounted. The WD-45 Allis Chalmers cultivator had a steel cross-bar that fitted across the front of the tractor about three feet off of the ground. This bar served a useful purpose in persuading reluctant cows to go to the barn. They usually responded well as they knew there was some additional feed at the end of the trip, but some animals occasionally were stubborn and determined to stay in the pasture and required chasing back and forth. But such behavior was easily countered when the tractor-cultivator bar was used. It was simply a matter of driving up behind the animal and giving her a gentle nudge with the bar. Had my father known of my technique he likely would have objected, but it was not often needed, and when it was it worked well!

The milk cows had to be brought in every night regardless of the weather. It was a pleasant task on sunny days, but a special problem on rainy ones. We did not own a rain coat when I was young, but when I reached teenage and acquired a bank account of my own, one of my first purchases was a heavy-duty rain suit which completely protected me from the rain and was used especially for going after the cows.

I have vivid memories of watching approaching thunderstorms build in the west and northwest and move toward our farm. Having gone through the tornado, we always watched approaching thunderstorms with some apprehension. The tremendous lightening flashes that reached from the green and black clouds that rolled and swept at the forefront of the system made strong statements about the power of the approaching storm. As the storm approached I would sit on the west porch or in the garage until it "declared" itself to either "go around" us or simply rain a lot. However, on many occasions we took temporary refuge in the storm cellar. After the storm front had passed it was considered safe to go after the cows, but that still often necessitated going in the rain.

The big pasture served purposes other than feeding the cows. It also was a place of entertainment and education for me. The open space was a wonderful place to ride the various ponies—especially Trigger, a beautiful little yellow and white "paint." He was a small horse, but he loved to run and I loved to ride him bareback at a full gallop. (We did not have a saddle!) Although spirited, he never bucked, and when my younger brother rode him Trigger always was very calm and gentle.

The pasture also was a place in which to "fool around." On the hillside there was a bare spot with exposed glacial rocks—apparently a failed gravel quarry. There were plenty of small rocks to pick through for possible pocketing and storage. I always was hoping for an arrowhead, but did not realize that the gravel quarry was an inappropriate site for such a find. However, I found a very nice piece of worked chert, the beginning of a spear point, in the creek bed.

There were numerous birds such as meadow larks and grassland sparrows—most of which I could not identify at that time. Most memorable is an upland plover that I flushed one summer day. Possibly this now rare species was nesting in the pasture that summer. In any case I remember the bird's long beak and legs, and beautiful grey-buff plumage with black specks. It was several years later that I learned the identity of this bird and importance of its presence as a symbol of a once abundant prairie species in that part of the country.

Going after the cows ended sometime after I went off to college. Carl, the owner of the pasture, died. The land was sold and the new owner plowed it and turned it into a soybean field. That is the way it is today. From my perspective, some consolation is that the new owner left a wide edge along the creek because it was too rough to plow. Over the years a band of trees reclaimed the creek bank. A few beaver dams periodically appear in the creek and then are moved as the ponds are silted full, but the beavers persist. Nuthatches, woodpeckers, and other birds are seen and heard in the trees. The cows are gone, but the deer are back. The last time I walked along the creek there were many deer tracks and a few saplings rubbed bare by bucks polishing their new antlers.

# MILKING

THE REASON FOR going after the cows was to milk them. Where the milking was done largely depended on the season. In summer we often milked outside, but in winter we always were inside the big barn. During my childhood we went through a succession of cows. They came and went for various reasons. Going usually was for poor performance; that is, low milk yield. Their characteristics and personalities varied. Blackie was black with yellow spots and short horns. She was one of the first to appear on the home place. Daisy, the afore mentioned Guernsey, stayed for many years. Daisy was more than just a source of milk. She also was a pet and since she tolerated being ridden sometimes served as a plaything. She was the typical gold and white characteristic of her breed and gave golden high butterfat milk—usually six gallons a day. Her many calves were our source of beef. We kept her many years and she was retired only after failing to either breed or to give enough milk to meet our needs.

We had one memorable Holstein heifer. She did not stay long because she was a high-jumper. She could clear a woven wire fence topped with two strands of barbed wire (a height of about five feet) with ease. Her favorite spot was inside a corn field located east of the house. We could never figure out why she abandoned a good pasture for the corn field, except she simply may have preferred young corn stalks to grass. In any case her rambles through the corn field were destructive and not appreciated. It was my job to chase her out. After doing it several times I got tough. I took the shot out of a shotgun shell and filled it with rock salt. The next time she got out I walked up behind her and "let her have it in the rear." She just switched her tail a couple of times and trotted ahead. Then I really got tough. I took one-half of the lead shot out of the shell. That time I stood about thirty yards away and peppered her rear end with the half-load. She jumped, ran ahead and out of the field, but showed neither damage nor memory of the event. She was back in the corn the next day. Dad finally gave up and sold her.

Milking was done by hand. After the cows were brought from the pasture they were put in a small lot or the barn. Often they were given grain—in part for nutrition and in part to keep them quiet. Some had halters with which to tie them, but others stood freely. Some were a bit difficult and would attempt to kick the milker while being milked. Even if they did not connect they often got dirt in the milk bucket or kicked the bucket over with a resulting loss of the milk. This was both dangerous and bothersome, so I attached "kickers" to the hind legs of these animals before sitting down to milk. The "kickers" were metal chains with a cup-like device that attached just above the "knees" and held the two hind legs loosely together. The result was that each of the legs was sufficiently immobilized to prevent the cow from kicking.

The next step was to clean the udder, better known as the "bag." Dad often just brushed away the mud, manure, and hay although a really bad case was washed with water out of the stock tank. This cleaning was essential, otherwise hay or dirt would fall into the milk. In fact some always seemed to do so, no matter how much you cleaned the animals. We always sat on the right side of the cow and usually on a stool. I had a special one constructed of a short piece of post and a cypress board nailed to the top. I just sat there, put my head against the cow's flank, grabbed the two near teats, and squeezed away. In the empty bucket the early streams made a "tink-tink"sound, but as the bucket filled it turned to a "swish-swish" as I milked in rhythm.

As the bucket filled I could smell the characteristic sweet odor of the milk as it wafted into the air.

Usually, milking was a rather pleasant experience, although it likely is more pleasant in memory then in reality. It always was done twice a day. The first milking was early in the morning and the second sometime late in the evening. This schedule was met regardless of the weather. One morning when it was fifteen degrees below zero the first spurts of milk froze on the side of the bucket. In the summertime I either swatted flies or sprayed the cow with fly spray before I started milking. Frequently I ducked the cow's flying tail, which passed at face height, as she attempted to remove the flies.

The cats, anywhere from one to six or eight, always provided a source of real joy during milking. Typically they were sitting either on the front porch or under the bushes in the yard when I emerged from the house with the milk bucket. They then came running and followed me down to the barn. While I milked they sat around the cows eagerly awaiting the coming feeding session. Some even learned to drink from a stream of milk squirted at them. They often got squirted anyway—so some learned to take advantage of it. (I also learned to squirt flies off of the cow's leg.)

After I finished milking the cow, I removed the kicker chains and turned her loose. In the summer the cows went out to the lot and pasture, but in winter they stayed in the barn overnight. I then picked up the milk pail(s) (three-gallon stainless steel or chrome plated pails) and walked to the house with the cats and dogs trailing behind or running ahead. The first stop in the yard was the cats' feed pan. The cats always rushed ahead, milled around my feet, and stood in the pan. The result was that one or more had part of the milk poured over them. That did not bother them as they or their siblings later licked it off.

From the cats, the remainder, and most, of the milk was taken into the house where it was strained to remove hairs, bits of dirt and hay leaves. In the old days we strained through multiple layers of cheese cloth, but later used commercial disposable strainers that did a more complete job. Today I shudder to know that so much crud got into the milk. Although we filtered out the particulate matter the bacteria likely went right on through. However, I doubt that any of us got sick from "barn germs" that might have gotten into the milk. Anyway, that was the routine way of handling the milk in those days. But, I am thankful for pasteurization today. After it was strained, the milk was assigned to pitchers for storage in the refrigerator or storm cellar and use on the table. The butter fat (cream) gradually rose to the top of the pitcher. It then easily could be skimmed off and used as cream or to make butter. The milk itself was used for drinking or making cottage cheese.

When we had an excess of milk it was processed by a "separator" in order to collect the cream for sale. Although efficient centrifugal separators were available they were fairly expensive and thus used by "larger" operations than ours. For years we relied on a simple water separator. It was a large open cylindrical tank about ten gallons in size and elevated on legs. The top had a removable inverted conical cover to which a strainer was attached. The milk was poured through the strainer into the tank and water was added to facilitate the passive separation process. A few hours later the milk-water mixture was removed by opening a cock located in the conical bottom of the tank. The cream, which was sitting on top of the mixture, followed the milk-water down and was gravity-collected into separate cream containers by the same process. The separator then was washed and readied for the next cycle.

Cream was stored in the refrigerator or storm cellar until taken to the creamery for sale at appropriate intervals. At that time there was a creamery in Mound City, owned by Cliff Broker, that bought both cream and eggs from individual farmers. Few in our community made major money from these commodities, but to most cream and egg money was a welcome supplement to other sources of income. The local creamery disappeared in the 1950s, due to a combination of factors including the advent of pasteurized milk in the local grocery stores, the growth of commercial poultry and dairy facilities, and the institution of stricter health regulations for dairy products. Small-scale production simply became unprofitable for both the farmer and the creamery owner.

MY BROTHER PAUL MILKING OUR FAVORITE COW,
DAISY

# DOING THE CHORES

OPERATION OF A general farm involved many more tasks than operation of a specialized farm. Among other things, each day, twice a day, the animals had to be cared for. We called these tasks "chores." The number, complexity, and physical demands changed as a kid grew. My first chore probably was gathering the eggs from the chicken house; a task previously described. The only dangers of this task were breaking an egg or being pecked by a hen who did not wish to move from the nest.

Egg gathering, "getting," gradually was supplemented by the task of feeding and watering the hens. Watering was simple except in the winter when I had to empty ice from the water pan. Usually I could simply invert the water pan and remove the ice cake. On other occasions I had to chop it out with an axe. Feed consisted of a mixture of table scraps, shelled corn or oats, and commercial laying mash. Usually there was only one main feeding each day and that was done in the afternoon or evening. Given that chickens have crops in which to store food, this frequency was adequate. In the summer the given food was supplemented by what the chickens found by foraging. Although there was a wire pen on the side of the chicken house, the chickens usually breeched it and succeeded in running loose around the place—much to the irritation of my mother and to the delight of the dogs and me. We always had a good excuse for chasing them: to get them out of the yard (that fenced part of the lawn that surrounded the house and was reserved for humans, cats and dogs). Mom had good reason because the chickens had no sense of where to drop their droppings. The sidewalk or porch was as good as the chicken yard. They also habitually scratched dusting spots in the flower gardens. The birds foraged from dawn to dusk pecking, scratching and waddling about. Probably they were good insect predators. Thus, they did not require much care during the summer. With the dogs nearby we did not worry about foxes and racoons getting them during the day and we closed the hen-house doors each evening after the birds had entered.

From chickens I was promoted to caring for the pigs, cows, and horses. Pigs is a generic description because we had feeder pigs and brood sows, and always a boar, each of which had special requirements. The feeder pigs were fed in the lot just east of the big barn. Dad had several troughs set aside for feed—mainly to keep it off the ground. The diet varied over the years, and with the age of the pigs, but the essentials were corn and nuggets (commercial supplement in pellet form). In the early years the corn was still on the ears and we simply scooped it out of the corn crib onto the ground. If the ground was wet the feed was put into troughs or carried into a shed with a dry floor. Dad allotted the amount of feed by experience rather than by strict formula. A certain number of pigs of a certain size got a certain number of scoops-full. His pigs always grew well and commanded good prices so apparently he was successful in the art of pig feeding. During the 1950s we changed from feeding ear corn to feeding shelled corn. At the beginning we took the ears of corn to the elevator in town and traded for shelled corn. Later in the 60s "picker-sheller" machines replaced pickers and the corn was delivered from the fields in shelled form.

Shelled corn was given better treatment than eared corn. Usually it was put directly into the troughs. Also Dad discovered various ways to improve its palatability. In the 1950s a popular supplement was buttermilk. It came from the store in huge sixty-gallon wooden barrels. It was thick and white—a thickened version from the dairies. We removed the top of the barrel, added water, mixed and then either gave it directly to the pigs or poured it over the shelled corn. "Soaked corn" was made by soaking the corn in five-gallon paint buckets full of water or water-buttermilk over night or for twenty-four hours. This softened the corn and presumably improved its nutritional qualities, although I suspect it primarily improved the culinary quality. In either case the pigs loved it.

The other main feed item was one of a variety of pig nuggets. The first I remember was of the Conkey brand sold by an old gentleman named Frank Collison whose store was in Maitland, Missouri. Apparently Conkeys tasted good because the dogs liked it at least as well as the pigs. My granddad had one dog that ate it so regularly that he was dubbed "Conkey": a gentle old black and yellow Shepard cross. The brands changed over the years— apparently with the rise and demise of the various companies and the rise and demise of the various feed salesman in the area. I think Walnut Grove and Moorman's are still extant, but many smaller companies are now extinct.

The nuggets were expensive, hence always given in a trough in measured amounts until the invention of the "automatic" or self-feeder. Trough feeding was somewhat dangerous and required adroitness and smarts. When the pigs saw me with the feed bucket they came running and squealing and began pushing against me. My strategy was to quickly put some feed in one end of the nearest trough. While they fought over that I ran to another trough and spread feed evenly along its length. When the pigs vacated the first trough I then had uninterrupted pouring. This scenario was carried out in all kinds of weather including rain and snow. Often the mud was six inches deep and mixed with pig manure. If the ground was frozen I often just threw the feed on the ground and ran. That approach worked fine.

Feeding methods for pigs changed significantly with the popularization (a euphemism for successful sales tactics by the supply stores) of self-feeders. Although there were a variety of shapes, all were (are) composed of a big reservoir with self closing doors arranged along or around the bottom. The reservoir was filled with feed which gravity-flowed to the doors. The pigs quickly learned how to open the doors to gain access—and then fed *ad libitum*. At least one of our feeders had noisy metal doors that clanged when the pig got full and pulled its nose out of the bin. This sound continued into the night. While lying in bed at night I could hear the pigs clang the feeder. On cold winter mornings one could hear the doors clanging on the neighbors' feeders over a mile away. Overall though, feeders were less aesthetically pleasing than the earlier method—if you enjoyed hearing the pigs chomp. I always found it satisfying to feed a hungry animal and watch and listen to it eat. My father often just sat and listened to the pigs eating. With the self-feeder you largely ignored the feeding itself and simply concentrated on keeping feed in the feeder.

Feeding beef cows awaited an age at which I could chop corn and handle baled hay: probably about ten or twelve. In the summer the cows grazed the pasture and only required daily or less frequent visits to check health, demeanor, and attitudes—plus the salt blocks and fences. In the winter they were moved into lots around the barns. Dad usually kept about twenty Shorthorn cows plus calves. The cows got along fine on a diet of hay fed twice a day. The hay usually was kept in the loft of the big barn and either tossed by "flake" or by whole bale to the ground below. The bales then were carried to the various feed bunks. We had two real bunks with slatted holders above the troughs, but also relied on old water tanks or the ground. I simply removed the wire or twine from the bale and tossed the pieces into the bunk for the cows to pull at while they ate.

The feeder calves and milk cows also got chopped or shelled corn. Chopped corn was the earlier version. I would carry a bucket of corn ears to the bunk, then use a corn knife (we now call them machetes) to chop the ear into pieces two to four inches long. Unlike horses, which carefully removed the corn kernels from the cob, the cattle would chew up the combined cob and kernels before swallowing.

Feeding calves was easy and one of my favorite jobs. The animals usually stood patiently and waited while I prepared the corn by laying an ear on the edge of the feed bunk and then chopping it into three or four pieces. They then moved up to the bunk only after I had stepped back. Particularly memorable are those cold snowy mornings when the red, or red and white, animals stood out against the white snow with "clouds" of breath coming from their frosted muzzles. The sparrows and starlings perched nearby awaiting some bits of grain while the bantam chickens foraged under and among the cows. Often it was dead quiet except for the occasional "moo" or stomp: a scene from a contemporary Currier and Ives print.

# SCHOOL

MOST OF MY early schooling was obtained at Bellevue Consolidated School. The name Consolidated arose from the fact that four surrounding one-room school districts (Dale Center, Minnesota Valley, Ross Grove, Liberty) were merged in 1913. The 1918 Atlas of Holt County shows the location of those schools. Liberty was located across the road from New Liberty church and Minnesota Valley was located beside a church of the same name. An unlabeled school, likely Dale Center, was located one mile west and one and one-half miles north of Bellevue. Ross Grove was located one mile south and one and one-half miles east of Bellevue. According to the cement plaque positioned over the front entrance, the Bellevue building was completed in 1922. When I entered the first grade in 1944, the total enrollment in all twelve grades was somewhat less than one hundred. Early in its history Bellevue likely was among the leaders of rural school districts. Unfortunately, changes in rural economics and the resulting social movement off the farm to the city ensured only a transitory existence.

The vacant school building still exists. A relatively large three story brick structure, it stands atop a large hill. This location provides occupants a commanding view of the country-side in all directions. Looking to the south from the upper floor of the school one can see across the Missouri River valley into Kansas located fifteen to twenty miles away. The ground floor contains a gymnasium sunk into the ground as a semi-basement—in later years called a "cracker-box" gym. The gym, which has a concrete floor, is about as small as possible and still capable of being suitable for competition. However, it was used regularly by all classes as a play area and for basket ball and volley ball games. Small, but adequate, spectator areas were located along both the north and south side. The area to the south actually was called a balcony. Behind the spectator area on the north were the twin coal (later oil) furnaces, the coal room (later the janitor's room), and separate bath-dressing rooms for girls and boys.

To reach the second floor one enters at either the north or south side of the building and climbs the central stairs to the large central hallway. Classrooms and offices were arranged along both sides of the hall. The second floor contained four class rooms: grades 1-3, grades 4-6, grades 7-8, and a science-math room. The administration office was located on the west between two of the class rooms. Across the hall between the other two class rooms is a room that originally served as the janitor's room, but later was converted to the school kitchen. At the south end of the hall there are two small rooms: one used variously as a storage area and sick bay and another used as the concession area where the junior class sold soda pop and candy.

A matched flight of stairs at the north end of the hall leads to the third floor which had two class rooms and a study hall-auditorium with a raised and curtained stage at the south end. The two class rooms typically were used for history and English classes and for commerce (business-typing-publications) classes respectively. There is still another narrow set of stairs beside the commerce room that leads up to a balcony that overlooks the hall and stage area below. Tucked beneath the balcony is a small room that was used as the school library.

The third floor was the province of the high school students. Within the study hall, desks were arranged in columns running north-south. The freshmen were seated to the east and the seniors to the west. In addition, the study hall had other desks and chairs used for school assemblies and community meetings. A well-used ping-pong table sat in the southwest corner and a phonograph on the corner of the stage. Two glass-fronted cases filled with sports trophies occupied the north wall on the east side. The stage at the south end, or front, of the room had a functional and quite nice black and orange-trimmed velvet curtain with a large orange "B" sewn into the top center. Behind the stage proper there were small prep areas for the plays and musical shows that were a regular part of the school program.

The school building is situated on the western side of a five-acre plot that was owned by the school district. This sizable plot allowed ample area for good play grounds and a reasonably functional soft ball diamond—limited largely by the row of trees that bordered right field. Two small homes were located at the far eastern edge of the plot. One housed the superintendent and his family and the other housed the custodian and his family. In addition there was an unused lean-to type of horse barn located at the bottom of the hill in the northeast corner of the plot. This was a relic of earlier days when some of the children still rode horses to school. White pine, red cedar, oak, and elm trees were scattered around the grounds. Someone had planted a weeping white birch beside the main driveway entry at the northwest corner. This tree and the flag pole at the middle of the front "lawn" served as the foreground for those entering the schoolyard. The overall effect was to create an idyllic setting for a school.

With few exceptions, school was an excellent experience for me. Classes were small enough that we knew each other reasonably well and the teachers could give each child their needed attention. My first grade teacher was Miss Bailey who I remember as "pretty and nice." I guess first grade went smoothly. There were "Dick and Jane " readers with stories about "Run Spot Run," alphabets, and numbers. The second year was far less pleasant. Miss Ginther (even her name sounds ugly) was a strict disciplinarian. I suspect I was a problem. Mom was still in bed with fever and Dad obviously was busy caring for her and trying to run the farm.

BELLEVUE CONSOLIDATED SCHOOL

The Bellevue Consolidated District was formed from four smaller one-room school districts in 1913. This building was completed in 1922 and served the district until 1964. At that time the Bellevue District joined the Mound City District. This photograph was taken from one of the later school annuals. The building was sold and used as a nursing home for several years and then as a private residence until it was abandoned. The building is still standing as of 2007. (Photo courtesy of Lillian Painter Wright)

Thus, I was relatively unsupervised at home and likely a bit lively at school. I do remember two incidents which earned me mild punishment. One was my using a crib-sheet on a spelling quiz. One of the words was Santa Claus. For that I deservedly had to "stay in" for at least one recess and possibly a noon-hour. The second was of a different type, and the punishment understandably justified. I had read a Dick Tracy comic strip in the local newspapers in which the main characters were FBI agents, so identified by the yellow FBI label on their caps. In the strip they knocked out the culprit with a blow by fist. The comic strip portrayed the blow to the criminal's jaw with a big "POW." I was impressed to the point where I made an FBI sign with crayon and yellow construction paper and pasted it to the front of my cap. When playing "cops and robbers" at recess I was the FBI agent and Jim Rosier, a neighbor boy, was the criminal. I "powed" him hard! He went crying to the teacher and I ended up missing recess for a week. Fortunately no permanent harm was done to anyone.

The first part of year three, which occurred after the tornado, was started at Lonesome school, but we moved to the Home Place in November and I continued the third grade at Bellevue with sour Miss Thompson. I have never thought about it before, but apparently there was a high turnover among elementary teachers.

In the fourth and fifth grades my teacher was Miss Edith Shipman. Sometimes wearing a long black dress with a white lace collar, she was a caricature of the spinster school teacher. But she was very dedicated to her job. About the fifth grade I discovered the school library and became an avid reader—I was called the "walking encyclopedia" by some. My curiosity also was fed by the traveling Book Mobile that appeared at about monthly intervals. That combination of teacher and library probably started me on the road to academia.

By the seventh grade I was lucky enough to have a rotund,

jovial, and excellent lady teacher by the name of Orrick Lenz. She daily copied onto the black board material from the study guide which we, in turn, copied into our note books. I regret that I never went to visit her in later years to tell how much she had influenced me. She appreciated my love of learning and really encouraged me and others. At about this time I developed an intense interest in natural history and decided to become a scientist of one sort or other—probably a zoologist.

Matriculation into high school was easy and enjoyable. I believe, with exception of coaches, I had the same teachers all four years. All of my teachers seemed to enjoy teaching and clearly were devoted to their jobs. Actually they probably had a really good situation. They had very few discipline problems, small classes, and good community support. The pay probably was as good as in surrounding districts, thus teaching likely was a pleasant experience for them as well as for the students.

There were six boys and two girls in my high school class and only three students in the class before us. Thus, the atmosphere was very family-like. We did not have band, football, or Future Farmers (vocational agriculture). Not having a football team was no major loss—it clearly preserved some of our joints. Band was replaced by chorus (with total participation) and with us all being farm kids we hardly needed a course in vocational agriculture. Most of us were fairly competent mechanics and animal husbandry persons by virtue of having gained on-the-job experience. The girls, of course, got equivalent experience in the home and some knew their way around the farm lot and field.

We were offered math through algebra and plain geometry, science through biology, four years of English (we read a Shakespeare play and wrote term papers every year), typing, general business, world and American history, health and driver training. We put on a play every year and all participated in multiple musical events. Everyone, unless physically disabled, played basketball and softball. There were both boys' and girls' teams and each was equally supported by the community. Women's lib was not a slogan—it was a reality, at least in sports and other school activities. Overall the atmosphere likely was far superior to that in most large schools, including rural ones, today.

It is hard to judge the quality of our education, but on the whole I think we got as good an education in the basics as did those in the larger area schools. Some of the high school teachers had Master's degrees and most had extensive experience. One music teacher, Mrs. Gottschalk, who unfortunately lasted only one year in the rural environment, had been a concert pianist in St. Louis. She apparently had been divorced recently and had brought her two children to the country either to "escape" or to one of the few available jobs. Unfortunately, the only available housing reasonably near the school also was relatively isolated and located about one and one-half miles south of the school down a dirt road (it is still dirt forty years later). The experience of getting about and staying warm during the winter must have been very trying for someone out of the large city. There were times when that road must have been impassable due to deep mud or snow. The house likely was poorly insulated, and probably not in very good condition. In fact she and her children may have been the last people to live in it. After her departure the house stood deserted for many years and then was torn down. So far as I know she was accepted by the community and I know we all were awed by her ability to play the piano. She always performed at least one solo at the various school events. However, I suspect the combination of gulf between former life style and the physical difficulty of living in that community contributed to her leaving after one year.

Most of the other high school teachers served the community well for several years. Raymond Mitchell, who drove daily from Fairfax, where he also farmed, served as coach, math and science teacher for at least my last three years of high school. Dorthea Sharp commuted from Mound City to serve as an excellent

English teacher for all of my four years, and Ginny Cardinell is remembered as a tough, but excellent, business teacher and publications director. Otis Jackson was the superintendent for many years. He also taught our history and driver's training courses and served as sponsor of the senior classes. A very gentle, but accomplished man, obviously he loved his job and likewise was loved by the students. The only run-in that I had with him was when another male student and I put a dead mouse in a girl's notebook. When she later opened the book during class there was a loud shriek as she jumped from her desk. That was a desired effect so far as Stanley and I were concerned, but Mr. Jackson viewed it with some seriousness. Our immediate punishment was to write an essay on the topic of mice.

I suppose the quality of our education might in part be judged by "how we turned out." Of the eight in our graduating class three boys went off to the University of Missouri that fall and all of us managed to survive at least four years. Larry Rosier became an engineer for McDonald Aircraft in St. Louis, Don Salfrank went into a business position, I think with Swift and Company, and I went on to do a PhD. Gene Miller married his high school sweetheart and became a very successful farmer. Stanley Crockett went to Tarkio College, but then fell in love and returned to successful farming and a construction business. Emmalea Seddon got a degree in Education from NW Missouri State at Maryville and became a teacher. Roger Smith and Anna Surritte went on to successful business careers. In those days a greater than fifty percent college entrance rate was unusual and those that did not go on to college succeeded well in their chosen occupations. My overall assessment is that we must have been adequately trained in high school and at home. At our 30th class reunion I was struck by the similarity of values that had persisted those thirty years. It seemed to me that we all were used to hard work, dedicated to family, reasonably happy with a "middle class" life, and believers in "God and Country"—not a loser in the bunch.

As in most small communities the school played a central role in the life of the community. The school house was the central community social place. We had the usual school programs at Christmas and other special occasions, and most members of the community came. They also attended sports events. An organization called the "Community Club," a local version of the PTA, worked with the teachers to provide food at sponsored events. A typical evening might be a gathering in the auditorium for a program and community sing from the *Golden Book of Song* followed by an adjournment downstairs into the hall for pie and coffee. The effect of "Community Club" was to create a close-knit atmosphere of mutual support for students, teachers and community.

My father, who served as president of the school board for many years, became good friends with many of the teachers. I think there likely was a similar relationship with the other board members, all local farmers, who had children in the school. I recall a perception of mutual respect and I think a feeling of genuine good will between the board and teachers. A teachers' strike never would have happened there and I think it never would have been necessary.

The only bad incident that I recall occurred after I had graduated. The school's lady cook, who was a good cook, but sort of a busy-body (she was the same person that wrapped her dining room table legs with newspaper) reported that she saw a male and female teacher "cozying up" to one another. He reportedly either had his arm around her or they were embracing. Anyway Dad and the members of the Board consulted and ultimately decided to fire the female teacher. Dad had the unpleasant task of delivering the letter. None-the-less the incident may reveal a certain prejudice against the female, and perhaps a willingness to take a rather drastic step on hear-say evidence. But, perhaps there were additional reasons, and I certainly never knew the full story.

Sports had a very significant role in school and community life. Although Bellevue was too small to have a football team we fielded respectable softball and basketball teams. When I first started school the girls played volleyball, but by the time I reached high school both boys and girls had basketball teams. Everyone in high school was on the teams—with the exception of one girl excused for health reasons and one girl excused for religious reasons. Although small in number, we did well in sports. We had respectable records against far larger schools every year that I was in high school. Most years the girls did better than the boys!

I started "suiting up" for basketball as a freshman and became a hero in one tournament game played in Mound City. We were playing Maitland in a close game, but apparently several of the upperclassmen had fouled out and I entered the game in the final minutes. I still was fairly short (5'2" according to the newspaper) so the opponents paid me little attention. That proved a mistake on their part. I stood under the basket, was passed the ball twice and made two baskets for four points. We won the game and I was written up as a hero in the local newspaper. Two years later I had reached 6'3" and 180 pounds and became a significant opponent. I averaged twenty-three points a game during my senior year and helped our team have a winning season.

I usually played very hard–so hard that I sometimes was sick. My worst mistake was eating one-half pan of Mom's newly baked cinnamon rolls a few hours before a hard game that was to be played in Rosendale some fifty miles away. About one-half way through that game I had one huge belly-ache. On the ride home in a snow storm, I had to ask Dad or Bud Nauman, whomever was driving to stop while I threw up. We lost that night—perhaps due to too many cinnamon rolls.

The basketball team was a real source of pride and a

tremendous binding force. Looking back I realize that success on the ball court carried over into many other things including my professional life. It built self-confidence, gave experience at both winning and losing, provided teamwork and friendship, and a continuing enjoyment of the game itself. I really never realized the importance of this positive sports experience until writing this.

Bellevue teams often had winning seasons and occasionally went to the regional tournament, but never beyond. None of our players ever won a significant sports scholarship, but some of them played at small colleges. I played intramural ball in my little spare time at the University of Missouri, and although I was reasonably good I never approached the sport seriously after high school. None-the-less, like most retired high school sports "stars," I look back on those days with great appreciation. Recently, while watching the film *Hoosiers*, a story about basketball in small town Indiana, I had the feeling that "I had been there."

In our community fast-pitch softball was much more informal than basketball. We played among ourselves at school every day that weather permitted, and competed with a few of the other area schools—particularly Maitland. Other than that it was summer-teams composed of locals and church teams. We usually practiced either at the school ground or, for at least one or two summers, in Gary Bruntmeyer's cow pasture. My favorite position was left-fielder because I liked to make (or try to make) running catches of high fly balls. Although we had some good players, most left the game behind after graduation from high school.

The Bellevue School is empty today. For financial reasons, the district was merged with the Mound City district in 1964. There were just too few children to support the twelve grades at Bellevue. Although I doubt that it was quite as good as I remember it, I feel strongly that the change was not wholly for the good. Admittedly there was no other choice, but if comparison were made of the atmosphere for learning with that of today I am reasonably confident that the "then" was better—in spite of the fact the present Mound City School is a very good one by regional standards. The student-faculty ratio was low, all faculty were well trained and loved teaching, the faculty and community were mutually supportive, most of the kids were serious, if not brilliant, and disciplinary problems were minor. Too few public schools of today can boast of that situation and America is weaker for it.

THE BELLEVUE BOARD OF EDUCATION –1956
OTIS JACKSON–Superintendent, LEROY ANDES, LESTER
METZGER, HARRY JACKSON,
KENNETH MILLER, ERNEST HESTER, RALPH ZACHARY

NEW LIBERTY BAPTIST CHURCH
The first church building was constructed and dedicated in 1876.
That building was demolished by a wind storm in 1885. The present
building was constructed in 1889.
(photographed June 2006)

# CHURCH

NEW LIBERTY BAPTIST Church can be described as a white rectangular wood frame box with a gable on top. The church, and the few ash trees that surround it, sit atop a ridge that rises from south to north. From the front door on the south one looks out across Mike Stoff's corn or soybean field as it dips into a valley through which passes a wooded stream. Beyond that, the hills, covered with a mixture of grain fields and small wood lots, and the intersecting streams lead the eye across the Missouri River valley to a view of the distant wooded hills of Kansas. A large, perhaps ten acre, well tended and grass-covered cemetery occupies the higher parts of the hill to the north and the lower part of the hill to the west. At the bottom of the hill to the east are a shed and two ancient privies—no longer used except by the wasps.

After entering New Liberty's front door one passes through a small vestibule (narthex), about twelve feet square, before entering the sanctuary. A brown carpet stretches between the green upholstered pews toward the front of the church. At the far front, behind the pulpit, hangs a blue, white, and gray print of Christ carrying the cross up the hill of Calvary. The print is framed in a beautiful hand carved and polished wooden frame of a design that I have seen no other place. The altar is flanked by an American flag on one side and a Christian flag on the other. Above and to the left is the "weekly report board" on which is posted attendance, offering, and lessons read. Below that board and to the left of the altar stands the piano and behind that two pews running parallel to the west wall. These two pews once held the youth choir, but today stand empty. An electric organ, dedicated in the memory of a former member, sits to one side of the altar.

The floor is carpeted, the ceiling paneled, and the air conditioned all due to the generosity of an admirer, but non-regular, former church member. The pews are even padded to provide comfort for the few people who still come to Sunday School and church. New Liberty is one of the few country churches still in existence in Northwest Missouri, but it is barely hanging on. Its gradual shrinkage is not due to loss of faith in the area, but to loss of population. Also the members are getting old (many in their seventies when I drafted this, but now in their eighties). Fortunately a few young families continue to worship there.

This church, in addition to the school, served as the other social center of my childhood. Shortly after moving to the Home Place we started going to church here. Mom has always been a church member, but I think Dad did not join until we had been in that neighborhood a few years. Our choosing that church likely was due to the fact that it is located only a mile from our house by road, and less by the "crow's route." The next nearest, Pleasant View Presbyterian, was three miles away over some then nasty roads.

New Liberty is a Southern Baptist church. Southern Baptists are relatively "fundamentalist" in their views and frown on most excesses (except smoking and eating). When I was a child the congregation had a full-time pastor, and was composed of a mixed-age congregation including several children. Our small, but viable and active, congregation met regularly. Sunday morning was devoted to Sunday School then church. Sunday evening was devoted largely to youth programs, and for a few years we had Wednesday night services—mostly singing and visiting.

The main attraction for me was that several other boys went to church there: Jerome Nauman, Jim and Larry Rosier, Gene

Miller, Stephen Taylor, and Sonny Van Orman. The parents were dedicated to providing us with religious instruction and social activities so the church became a strong part of my life. Admittedly it was primarily for social rather than theological reasons.

None-the-less I owe a huge debt to those wonderful men and ladies who served as teachers and friends. Valetha Miller, the mother of one of the other boys, and Dorthy Quador served as Sunday School and Bible School teachers during my earlier years there. All youth activities (classes) were held in the church basement—a space only about thirty by sixty feet in size. Youth of various ages were divided into three classes that met on the east side of the basement and separated by curtained petitions from the men's class held at a table on the west side. It must have been noisy, but I do not remember it as so. What strikes me as interesting is that men and women had separate classes. The women met upstairs in the sanctuary. I guess it was the denominational pattern. Today (1980s) they meet together—probably because the total attendance is fewer than twenty adults.

We used regular "quarterlies"(lesson books that covered a period of three months) for our lessons. The teacher led us through the printed lesson. I was neither especially interested nor bored so I guess the teachers were successful in keeping our attention. They were successful in influencing our lives. As far as I know all of the kids that I grew up with still practice religion, although some of us have switched denominations, and most, if not all, have passed it on to their children.

I remember three of the several preachers that served during my childhood. The Reverend Ivan Herring was a big soft-spoken man who was rather quiet, undistinguished, loving and highly respected. He was a rather even-tempered, level-headed sort whose sermons must have been bland, but effective. I do know where he went, but I trust to another call.

He was followed by a smallish, black- haired fellow who had a pretty blond wife and three small skinny daughters. I sometimes wondered if Frank Bullock and his family got enough to eat. I am sure the pastor's salary was not great though it likely was sufficient. The church maintained a parsonage in Mound City that was provided as part of the pay package so at least the family got decent housing. My father usually gave the preacher a cured ham or other meat each year. Frank and Peggy left for Alaska in the early 1950s where at last word he still was serving.

The last to come before I went off to college was Everett Branson and his wife Rosalie. They came out of south Missouri—the hilly part. He was a tall, partially bald, slim man in his late forties or early fifties. She was short, stocky, and perhaps a bit younger. Most memorable are his big hands and big feet and her cheerful countenance. They came with few material goods. The old car, probably at least ten years old, was faded blue with a cracked rear window. His suit was well-worn, brown and ill fitting. Apparently he had worked in a shoe factory before "getting the call." My impression was that he had relatively little formal education, but intense conviction, humbleness, and dedication to basic Christian beliefs.

Reverend Branson's sermons were loud, and passionate; very much fundamentalist, but he lived as he taught. He would come to work in the fields at haying time, I guess for fellowship, but I suspect that he often was paid for his help. In one way his life was a series of small tragedies. While serving the church he was involved in a terrible traffic accident. He was driving south on the blacktop state road located two and one-half miles east of the church one summer afternoon. This road, like all in the vicinity, is hilly. Reverend Branson was at the bottom of a small hill when another car, traveling very fast, came over the hill and hit his car head on. Apparently it was a glancing blow as neither Branson nor his car were badly damaged, but the other car was traveling so fast it split down the middle killing the tenant-farmer who was driving. Sadly he was the father of several small children. No ticket was issued as it was judged to be the other man's fault, but clearly Reverend Branson was greatly affected.

One funny incident took place at Bud Nauman's dinner table. I was helping with haying at the time and we were having dinner (the noon meal). My dad, Bud, and his son, Jerome, the Bransons and a few others were at the table. During the conversation we got off on the subject of knives. Dad had his castrating knife with him and it was being passed around the table. A feature of castrating knives is an L-shaped blade used for cutting the spermatic cords of pigs and calves—those unlucky enough to be subjected to the operation. When it was passed to, or near, Mrs. Branson she asked what that L-shaped blade was for. Dad and Bud were too polite to explain the true use, so one of them said, "It's a pop bottle opener." That ended the explanation.

The last time I saw the Bransons was in the early 1960s when we visited them in South Missouri. They were living near Rolla, having left New Liberty a few years previously. We drove off the highway, then down a twisting country oil road, then back in a pasture to a small weathered house sitting among the hickory trees. Inside the wall-paper was faded to match the well-worn furniture. Rosalie was jovial as ever despite suffering from an illness (nature undisclosed) and as appreciative of the "Lord's care" as ever. I was deeply impressed by the apparent joy of living, mutual devotion, and trust in the Lord of this materially poor couple. I heard no complaints, only thankfulness for the blessings they did have—including our visit to them. They taught a good lesson.

I still visit New Liberty once or twice a year. The cemetery gradually has been modified over the years—most recently by removal of the grass-filled woven-wire fence that surrounded it and replacement with an attractive white plastic one. Use of herbicides makes the upkeep of the cemetery and fence line much easier, but in the process the beautiful native prairie flowers that I saw as a child have been destroyed. I have no legitimate voice in the matter, but I morn that loss.

Although there are some new faces at church on Sunday morning only a few of the old faces remain.  In a matter of years those voices and faces will be memories of the still aged and younger. Only the spirits of the bathrobe- and towel-clad shepherds who walked up the aisle on Christmas eves will remain as will the echoes of the voices that praised on Sundays.  Perhaps no other institution or building can so profoundly remind us of our transiency on earth—a thriving, living community passes because of economic forces beyond the control of those involved.  Unless young families suddenly start flocking into the surrounding countryside New Liberty, like Minnesota Valley, Pleasant View, and Church of the Brethren, also will soon stand empty and possibly then disappear.  The only thing to mark its presence will be the remains of a foundation and the tomb stones in the cemetery that surrounds it.

# JOE

I NOW LIVE in a middle-class neighborhood in a middle-sized Midwestern city. On the occasion of my daughter's birth several years ago I told my wife that I regretted that she would grow up in such a homogeneous neighborhood lacking the type of characters that I had known as a boy. (Subsequent events would prove me wrong as we discovered a few in the vicinity). Most of those living in my boyhood community were reasonably successful farmers who attended church fairly regularly, had children, supported the local school and stayed out of trouble. Most had notable, admirable characteristics and fell within my perception of normal. On the other hand there were a few who either fell outside of this mold or played a special role during my childhood. Some I knew so little about that I cannot provide a useful description much beyond their names and a few outstanding behavioral characteristics, but others left a strong impression.

Among them was Joe, a traveling farm laborer, who went from farm to farm as needed. He probably was a product of World War II, was without a steady job and perhaps lacked the requisite education to hold a one. He was sandy haired, lean, usually clean-shaven, in his late thirties or early forties, soft spoken and self effacing. His home, if he truly had one, was in Mound City, but he stayed as a hired man on various farms in the community. He was a hard worker, but was a mild alcoholic. That fact usually preceded him on the job. He worked for a neighbor, we will call him Tom, for several years. Although Tom had three boys, they were fairly small. Joe slept in the north room upstairs—beyond the boys' bedroom. The north room was unheated and probably hot in the summer as I think there was only one window in he north side—certainly no cross ventilation. And I faintly recall bare lathes without plaster on part of the wall. It was an adequate, but certainly not luxurious place.

The three boys, who at that time ranged in age from about eight to twelve years, discovered one of Joe's whiskey bottles hidden on a rafter in the garage. Apparently the oldest was knowledgeable about medicine for they placed a large dose of Epson salts in the bottle and then replaced it on the rafter. The outcome (no pun intended) was never discovered, but the boys apparently had fun telling their friends about their trick. I doubt that their parents approved.

Tom was well aware of Joe's drinking habit, but tolerated it because it was not a severe enough problem to affect his work. Tom figured he sweat alcohol (sweated it out). However, Tom had other subtle ways of dealing with the problem. Joe developed a toothache, probably due to a badly decayed tooth. Tom took him to a dentist who proceeded to give Joe some novocaine and extract the tooth. That night he obviously was suffering some discomfort and apparently had tried to deaden the pain with a noticeable dose of the hidden spirits. Either after dinner, or just before bedtime, Tom asked Joe how he felt. The reply was something like, "Not so good." Tom then said, "Joe, I'm really glad you do not drink whiskey. They tell me that whiskey and that stuff the dentist gives you to reduce the pain is really deadly. Apparently you go to sleep and never wake up." It is unknown how well Joe slept that night, but apparently that incident did not cure his habit.

Joe worked for my dad for a short time. One sunny, but frosty, fall morning, the day he was to start work, we saw him coming up from the barn shortly after sunrise. He walked to the front door and softly knocked. Dad invited him in for coffee or breakfast, and asked who he had ridden out from town with so early in the morning. "Oh," Joe said, "I came out last night and just got in the barn and slept in the oat bin."

The last I heard of Joe he had been hit and killed by a car while walking along the highway one dark night. It was speculated, but never proven, that he was drunk and had wandered onto the road. Clearly his story is a sad one. Superficially he could have been considered the town drunk, but at the core he was a kind and decent individual. Unknown events, perhaps the war, or persons, at sometime in his life had somehow altered that core and led to his less than ordered life. I have no idea where he was buried, but I suspect it was in an unmarked pauper's grave in one of the local cemeteries.

# CARL

THE LARGE WHITE house, which was ultramodern for the time with full bath and central heat, guarded the entrance to the farm. The house sat on a rise behind a lawn that stretched to the road two-hundred feet to the west. It was surrounded by trees and gardens: four tall scotch pines and several Colorado blue spruce to the west with assorted ornamental bushes scattered around the sides. An open porch, supported by concrete pillars, curved around the west and south sides. A screened porch, which occupied the southeast corner, opened to a concrete deck over which arched a trellis covered with Wisteria. The garden at the southeast corner of the lawn was filled with roses, iris and numerous other flowers. The south lawn sloped to a drive way lined on both sides by tall catalpa trees. A large vegetable garden lay beyond the driveway and joined the south pasture. To the north there was a large orchard of assorted apple trees.

Behind the house there were three barns (a very large dairy barn, a hay barn, a corn crib), scale house, chicken house, storage shed, wash house, brooder house and a garage. All were painted white and kept in immaculate condition. The north side of the lawn-orchard area was bordered by a windbreak of two rows of northern white pine trees. A few hundred yards to the east Wildcat Creek formed a natural border as it ran southwest diagonally across the field and crossed under the road one-quarter mile south of the house. The south pasture, perhaps five acres in size and triangular in shape, was the home of two or three brindle mixed-breed or Jersey cows. There was a distinct aura of wealth and elegance about the place.

The farm was occupied by three siblings—all probably in their mid-fifties when I first met them. Carl Nauman, the man of the house, was provided company by his two sisters Stella and Clyda (Clydie as we knew her). Stella was an invalid who occupied a bed in the southwest corner of the first floor, but Clydie was full of energy and apparently cared for the other two. My recollections of Stella are vague—only that of a faceless person in the distant room—as she died shortly after we moved into the neighborhood. I never knew the history of the family or ever found out why the three siblings ended up living together in relative wealth. Apparently there were no ex-spouses. The three of them largely kept to themselves. Aside from their renters' families, I think they had little social life. They never participated in school or church activities, and having no offspring were not interested in the local sporting events. Carl's apparent joys were the farm, gardens, orchards and his hobby of making wine from his Concord grapes. Occasionally he would invite Dad to sample the latest batch.

We got to know Carl and Clydie well as they were our nearest neighbors to the north and because Dad had rented and farmed much of their land, including the big cow pasture, as well as served as friend and "servant" for many years. However, it was not until 1946, the year of the tornado, when we bought the Home Place, which adjoined Carl's land, that we began to make frequent visits to Carl's house.

Carl seemed intent on having the best that money could buy. He always kept a late model Oldsmobile 98 in the garage even though neither he nor Clydie could drive. They made fairly frequent trips to town with either Dad or Glen Nauman, another renter, acting as chauffeur. Carl always sat in front while Clydie always sat in the left rear seat. They were fairly generous with the car and loaned it to Dad to take Mom to the hospital in Saint

Joseph the night my brother was born. That perhaps was due in part to the fact that Dad had driven Carl to St Joseph, to the doctor, to get a broken collar bone set. The mules unexpectedly had jumped forward when Carl was standing in the back end of a wagon and had thrown him out onto his face and shoulder. Apparently the local doctors could not set the broken bone, so they had to take him the fifty crooked miles of old Highway 275 to St Joseph.

Television first came to our part of the country in the early 1950s. Carl quickly bought a console powerful enough to receive "snow"-filled pictures from Kansas City channels 4 and 5. Our family spent many Saturday nights watching TV in Carl's living room. The programs usually were "Hit Parade" (Snooky Lansen, Rosemary Clooney), "Fireside Theatre," and, of course, wrestling.

Both Carl and Clydie passed away in the late 1950s or early 1960s—the sequence and specific time forgotten. The survivor had a general sale of the household goods. I bought the beautiful cherry cabinet Philco radio-phonograph console for $5.00. It still functions forty years later—a testament of its quality. The land was sold to multiple owners. Although Dad wanted the big pasture that adjoined our farm he somehow missed getting it. The result was that the pasture, the one from which I fetched the cows, was plowed and put into row crops. The barns were abandoned. For a time the house was rented, progressively damaged, and then abandoned. Gradually the buildings deteriorated, the orchard invaded by grass and weeds, and the apple trees broken and dead. The big dairy barn stood for nearly forty years while the shingles blew off and the rafters rotted away. At the time I write this the barn has collapsed except for a shed roof on the south end. Only a few piles of rotted hay and scattered pieces of harness remain as signs of the horses and cows that occupied the barn. Rusty fragments of equipment are scattered among the fallen boards.

The house still stands, but all of the windows are gone, the floor has collapsed, and the plaster is falling from the walls. In the garden, now filled with 4-6 inch diameter trees, a few daffodils and surprise lilies bloom as reminders of the hand that put them there fifty years ago. In another fifty, there will be no signs of this once elegant farmstead. Even the names will be forgotten.

## AFTERWARD

I drafted this recollection in the 1980s. I am sorry to say that my predictions came true. The then current owner of the farmstead passed away and the heirs sold the place. One early spring, while on a visit, we were driving home from town. Looking ahead we spied a huge black cloud of smoke rising from near the Home Place. Our apprehension grew as we drew nearer, but as we turned the corner from the north we realized that the fire was at Carl's place. The new owner was burning the house and other old buildings. We stopped as they went up in flames and watched as a smoking mother racoon jumped out of a burning pine tree and scurried off into the remaining grass. All that was left standing was the concrete porch columns and the foundations. A few months later these were bulldozed to a pile near the creek. Surprisingly the pine windbreak was left intact, as was a length of the berry patch growing along the road. However, in another year that also was gone and the homestead now is covered by a grain field and a few scattered brush piles.

# EVERETT

ALTHOUGH I HAD heard stories about him, the first time I saw Everett Mann I still was surprised, and even a little shocked, by his appearance. It happened one summer afternoon when I was helping a neighbor harvest hay from a field that Everett owned. Shortly after the job had begun, Everett came driving into the field. His pickup, an eighteen-year old 1936 Ford, should have been consigned to the salvage yard several years previously. Both bumpers were hanging at an angle and barely attached to the body. The right rear fender was gone exposing a tread-bare tire. The doors were tied shut with short pieces of one-quarter inch sisal rope. The paint was about gone, and the surface of a once bright blue truck now was a mixture of gray and faded blue blotches atop the dirty black undercoating. Everett's clothes had much the same appearance as the truck's paint. They were blue jeans and a chambray shirt, but the spots were caused by the addition of foreign materials instead of the wearing away of the original dyes. The black spots on his clothing were offset by the white of his inch-long beard and the white rubber trim of his tennis shoes. In his left hand he held a six-pack of warm Pabst Blue Ribbon beer which he proceeded to offer to the haying crew—most of whom were tee-totalers.

At the time of our first introduction Everett probably was in his mid-fifties, but his appearance made it hard to judge his age. According to the adults in the field, he was extremely bright, but obviously very eccentric. When in his early teens he was considered both witty and very promising. According to legend, his knowledge of mathematics and classical writings was outstanding—at least by local standards. At the age of seventeen he was auditing books for local businesses. At age thirty he was owner of a half-section of farm land and very prosperous.

Then something happened. Over time he changed from a person of ambition into what some locals called a bum. Others called him a hermit and a few considered him a mild "psycho." The farm, while remaining productive, had gradually deteriorated. The buildings were unpainted, the fences sagging, and the weeds unmown. In addition to the crop land, which he rented to a neighbor, he kept a herd of cattle that roamed a pasture and adjacent wooded area. Their care and supervision seemed to be minimal. Rather than fat, sleek and docile like those in my father's herd, Everett's were skinny, variegated and wild. Reportedly, about half were intact bulls that repeatedly breeched the sagging fences to mix with the neighbors' cows or raid the adjacent corn fields. Needless to say this caused considerable hard feelings and in some cases they were chased back toward Everett's with the blast of a shotgun.

It was rumored that he kept most of his supposedly extensive fortune in one of the local banks. Clearly he did not spend any except when he went to town once or twice a month for food and liquor. He made known his drinking habits in some interesting ways. When our community had a benefit auction for the "Polio Drive" he contributed a lamp constructed from a make-it yourself kit. The interesting thing about the lamp was that the base was a half-gallon corn whiskey jug. This lamp caused considerable comment, but did not command a high price. I bought it for fifty cents.

His drinking eventually got out of hand. There were no local support groups or agencies to help him deal with the problem. He was arrested several times for driving under the influence. Finally the judge suspended his driver's license, but Everett accommodated beautifully. When he wanted to go to town he simply drove his tractor as he did not need a license to drive it on a public road!

Aside from the hay field meeting, I had only one other interaction with Mr. Mann. This occurred one evening of November 1955. Three other boys and I were selling Christmas cards and wrapping paper in order to supplement the treasury of our high school junior class. This money was to help finance our senior trip. We had exhausted most of our sales prospects, but then thought of Everett. We also wanted to have a little fun, so called on him.

We knocked three or four times before he came to the door. He let us in and then asked us to introduce ourselves. After the formalities we were led into his living room and each of us was assigned a chair. He plopped down in a dirty red couch which was littered with movie and "true story" magazines. A table at the end of the couch held a massive *Webster's Unabridged Dictionary* and several books by early American writers such as Emerson and Hawthorne. Noting my interest in the books he reached up and took a typewritten manuscript (a typewriter sat on an adjacent table) from the Emerson. It was titled "Excerpts from the Sermons of Emerson," and bore the subscript, "Compiled by Mr. Everett Mann this day of June 25, 1955." He then proceeded to read it. Although the content was beyond our understanding, we sat and listened, trying hard to stifle our ensuing laughter, as he read with great enthusiasm. As soon as he was finished, he folded the paper, put it away, and then asked us to state our business. With much exaggeration we described our wares. Either our salesmanship was good, or he was kind-hearted, for we sold him three boxes of our best cards. It is unlikely that he ever used them and I suspect they sat by the Emerson and Webster's for a long time.

Everett did not take Emerson's sermons very seriously. He was an admitted atheist who reportedly delighted in challenging those few ministers who periodically visited him. According to the local gossips, every time a minister tried to engage him, Everett would start quoting from the Bible and recite "biological evidence" that there is no God, using language of "a college professor" to make his point. Although the Baptist church was only about a mile from his house he apparently never attended.

On the other hand he reportedly was not afraid of death. According to one of his farm tenants Everett said that he was ready to die "any day." He had his grave site picked out. It was located in the timber just east of his house. The site was covered with grass and surrounded by a sagging wire fence. In addition he had picked out and designated the songs to be sung at his funeral: among them *Home on the Range* and *This Old House.* He had a recording of each that he wanted played when he "passed on."

Interestingly, and probably happily, a few years after my encounters with Everett he found a lady who appreciated some of his better qualities. I am told that he was visiting the Seattle World's Fair where he met up with his cousin Kate Mann. At age seventy-seven he married her. The ceremony had to be performed in Canada because Washington statutes prohibited marriage of first cousins —regardless of age. They returned to the home farm where they lived for several years before moving to Mound City.

Like many of the others in this story, nothing remains of Everett's farmstead. A few years ago my brother and I visited the woods that stood east of the house and salvaged a couple of beautifully figured wine bottles from the trash dump.

# LOUIE

MY NEAREST NEIGHBOR, Louie Kunkel, stood over six feet tall—mostly bone and no fat. His usual dress was faded blue bib overalls, blue cotton shirt, work shoes and striped railroad hat. I never saw him in a suit; however, occasionally he went to church so perhaps did have one. He was easy going, kindly, unexcitable. Although not particularly religious he rarely, if ever, cussed or spoke ill of others.

He and his wife, Stella, probably were in their mid-fifties when I first met them. They lived across the road and across the creek to the west of us. Their house was located on the side of a hill overlooking two small creek valleys to the east and south. The small wood frame structure had only five rooms: kitchen-dining room, living room, two very small bedrooms, and a pantry. However it had a screened-in porch along the east side and an unscreened porch on the south. Painted white, roofed in green shingles, it nestled under box-elder trees affording its inhabitants an idyllic view of the valleys below. Heat was provided by a giant green and ivory cook stove in the kitchen and a standard brown stove in the living room—both wood and coal burning. Water was carried by three-gallon enameled or galvanized buckets from the hand pump located sixty feet down the hill to the east. There was a sink in one corner of the kitchen, but no running water or bathroom. The kitchen windows faced north and opened onto the flower garden-orchard that was planted to a mixture of peonies, blooming shrubs and a few apple and peach trees. The opening to the storm-root cellar stood in the northeast corner of the lawn.

Although it was simple, many a "yuppie" couple of today would covet living in this little house in this lovely location.

The out buildings were many years weathered. Most lacked paint and were patched with bits of tin and tar paper. The windows of the chicken house were protected with bits of rusted chicken wire over which were stretched faded feed sacks. The old cowbarn had a small hay shed at the west side whereas the east side was an open loafing area and "milking parlor." The battered milking stool lay beneath an old sack that was stuffed between a post and the yellow-gray faded walls. At milking time this area was occupied by three or four spotted, skinny cows that were adequately, but not over fed. The small lot in front of the cow barn opened into a larger one which connected to the lane and small pasture that partially covered the valley south of the buildings. Notably the fence rows were filled with coral berry and other bushes and small trees that supplemented the sagging wire fencing.

Louie's place was about a quarter of a mile from the county road to the east, but was separated from that road by Wildcat Creek. It also was one-half mile from the nearest road to the south. To reach the house by car one had to drive from the south over a private dirt road that wound its way through the fields and across a plank bridge over a small creek. The road then led through the pasture, up a lane, and into the greater lot below the house. This route was impassible in bad weather. Consequently Louie often walked to our house to get a ride into town during the winter or after a rain storm.

To reach the county road and the mail box to the east he followed a dirt path leading across the lots and field, then crossed the creek and continued on out to the road (now called Ironwood Road) that ran past our house. The English would call it a footpath. The creek-crossing was appropriately elaborate. The banks were over ten feet high at the crossing site. Louie simply used a spade to cut steps down both sides of the stream. He laid a two by ten-inch board over the stream to serve as a crossing and attached one end of the board to a heavy steel wire. The wire led to a post high on the bank. This wire anchor prevented the "bridge" from washing away during high water. This path was the well-traveled route between our house and Louie's.

Louie and Stella farmed eighty acres which they had inherited from Louie's father, Harve. Although Louie may have done the farming himself at one time, he was renting the crop land to someone else during the time that I knew him. The tilled part of the property probably was less than sixty acres and corn was the usual crop. The assorted cows provided milk, cream, and butter. The excess cream provided a modest source of income. They also kept several hens for eggs which they also sold to the creamery on Saturdays.

The very large garden located between the cow barn and hen house was the object of most of Louie's agricultural attention. The garden provided a major source of food—as did gardens of most country folk in those days. However, Louie always was eager to share his produce. The small orchard yielded a few apples, peaches and plums. In addition wild mulberries, goose berries, and black berries were harvested for pies and preserves. Eighty acres was a small farm, even in the 1950s-60s, yet it seemed to provide Louie and Stella with sufficient income to allow them a comfortable living. They had a car, but not a television while on the farm. That came later when they moved to town. Louie was not known as an aggressive farmer, but none-the-less seemed to enjoy life and prosper in his own way.

Louie had some virtues that particularly endeared him to me: he hunted, fished, and liked to talk about such activities. Also he let me hunt in his superb large wild blackberry patch located along the ditch west of his house. It was an ideal arrangement both interest- and space-wise. To get to the blackberry patch I had to pass near the house so a visit, or at least an exchange of greetings, was inevitable. My usual route was to cross the creek, hunt in the grass and brush around the old "ox-bow" lake in the bottom field, than walk up the hill to the house. I usually stopped to say "Hi," see if he wanted to hunt, or be invited in for coffee, conversation and whatever "sweets" Stella had to offer from the kitchen. Memories of specific visits are gone, but there remains a montage of sitting around the oil-cloth covered round kitchen table by the big green and cream colored cook stove or of sitting in the living room by the brown heating stove that had mica windows on the fire box.

A piano sat in the living room against the southeast wall. Stella had it covered with knick-knacks. The most memorable was a rattlesnake ash tray—atrocious, but a good conversation piece. A long narrow photograph of Louie's World War I army group hung on the north wall behind the stove. Apparently he had never left the U.S., but none-the-less was a proud veteran and active member of the Hardin Story American Legion post in Craig, Missouri.

The memories of that house are very warm ones. These kind and gentle people were representative of that group who are not "community leaders" or particularly successful in monetary matters, but who none-the-less make those essential contributions of being friends to their neighbors, providers for their family, and self-sufficient citizens.

Louie and Stella left the farm and moved to town sometime in the 1960s. I did not see much of them then as I was off to college and got back home only once or twice a year. The farmstead stood unused for many years and I often, when home, hunted by myself or walked with Dixie, my wife, around the old buildings and along the weed grown fences. Stella died quite unexpectedly a few years after they had moved to town. Louie remained in Mound City for only a year or two and then moved to Loveland, Colorado. There he met another lady friend, Edna as I recall, a native of the Sand Hills of Nebraska. They never married, probably for economic reasons, but shared each other's company for several years. The last letter I received from him contained a photograph of Louie holding a large sugar beet that was grown in a field near their apartment. At that time he was in his seventies and still looking good. He and Edna actually drove back to Missouri one or two times to visit family and friends. I managed time to drive down to visit them while attending a meeting at Fort Collins. A couple of years later Louie died.

The farm passed to his daughter, Gladys Flake who lived about twenty miles away. Nothing much changed for a few years, but then the north part of the farm was sold to the neighboring farmer. The inevitable happened—the buildings were bulldozed to the ground and burned, and the fence rows removed. Today there are only a few pieces of crockery scattered in the field to mark the location of Louie's place. Eventually those also will be dispersed and lost.

The fate of Louie's place, like that of many others in the community, provides a rather sobering lesson. The hard work and effort by Louie and Stella to build their farm served them well, but did not last long beyond their life time. That fact is partly the fault of those who remain, but also is testimony to the reality that few of the average person's physical accomplishments will be long remembered. It seems likely that all of mankind's works, even those built of stone and steel, eventually will meet the same fate. The archaeological and historical record certainly suggests it. The messages are many. Be aware that we must savor, enjoy, appreciate and recognize those good things we have now. Lives and circumstances of all inevitably will change. It is good to treasure those memories of joys in the past and to measure the present against the past, but it is even more important to capture the fullness of the present.

# DUCKS

AT ABOUT AGE twelve I discovered ducks and duck hunting. This discovery was due in part to geography and in part to the passion of some of our neighbors for the sport. As the old saying goes, "I was in the right place at the right time." The right place because our farm is located only six or seven miles north of the Squaw Creek National Wildlife Refuge which in the1950s gave temporary haven to about a half million mallards each October and November. Also, for reasons not clear, the fields to the east of our house, particularly the high ridges of the Morris Place were favorite feeding grounds for the ducks. The right time because mallard populations were very high at that time, due apparently to good nesting conditions in the North and adequate food in the winter.

Our neighbors Louie Kunkel, Loren Pender and David Painter all were avid hunters who often hunted on our place because of the high use by ducks. Louie once or twice gave us a duck to roast, but we found it "gamey," apparently because Mom did not have the first idea of how to cook a duck. She is of the "cook it until it is tender" school, which is exactly opposite of what the average duck requires: cook it until it is just done, pink and juicy. Fortunately, my experience ultimately extended beyond those first culinary attempts.

What probably was the pivotal event occurred one fall day when I noticed several very large Canada Geese circle and then alight on the hill east of the house. I decided to take my BB gun and sneak up on them. They saw me well before I got close, rose slowly and flew off honking loudly—literally honked off. Two people also were "honked off." My neighbors had been sitting in a blind waiting for a shot at these rare and most desired of waterfowl trophies; however, my approach ruined that possibility. Their reaction, to my dad at least, was a mixture of amusement and irritation, but they apparently soon forgot the incident.

My first real duck hunt occurred either later that fall or the next one. One afternoon Louie and Dad took me out onto the "twenty," a twenty acre field located northeast of the house. Louie had his Model 1897 Winchester 12 gauge pump, Dad had a 22 caliber rifle (not a true duck hunting gun), and they gave me Louie's single shot 16 gauge. The afternoon was cold and cloudy and there was a bit of snow on the ground. We hunkered down below a dam, in among the tall fox-tail grass and weeds that lined a small ditch. About 3 or 4 PM a large bunch of ducks appeared. They seemed to be landing up the hill from us, but were circling and flying just above our heads when Louie yelled "now!" I jumped up and shot into the bunch, as did the others. Somebody killed a hen mallard, but being good instructors they thought that I probably had hit her. I still remember those speckled feathers on the head and breast, the blue speculum on the wing, the orange feet and the blackish bill of that particular hen, but I do not remember the return to the house, dressing the duck, or eating it. However, that experience converted me into a duck hunter.

The only problem was that I did not have a gun and I guess Dad thought I was too young for one. Providence solved that problem. Dad had let some duck hunters from St Joseph dig a "duck pit" in one of our fields. A pit was simply a blind made by digging a hole about three feet deep and two by four feet wide and then partially covering it with corn stalks and weeds for camouflage. Many farmers would have charged a fee, but Dad let them do it for nothing. However, being grateful, one of the hunters, a doctor from Stanberry, appeared on the porch one evening a few days before Christmas with a bolt-action, three-shot, 20 gauge Kessler shotgun for me. It was about as cheap as was made, but I was thrilled. I had a gun! The rest of that winter I used it for rabbit hunting, but I was looking forward to the next fall.

Early in the fall I shot a couple of hen mallards off a pond, but the real hunting did not begin until our first snow storm. That late November night it was snowing when I got home from school. I quickly got into my hunting clothes (blue jeans and a brown hunting coat which I had earned by selling garden seeds) and quickly went up to the Morris hill east of the house. By the time I got there it was snowing big wet flakes and getting nearly dark, but the ducks were landing in great numbers just across the fence row to the east. They paid little attention to me and I crept close, shot into the bunch, and dropped one hen mallard. That was tremendous sport to hunt in a storm—real duck-hunting weather.

The next day there was several inches of snow on the ground and ducks everywhere. Some of my most vivid memories are of that day: the white undersides of the ducks against the bright blue sky, and the green heads of the drakes as they waddled down the corn rows toward me. All I had to do was hide in the grass and let them walk in my direction. In that first year I was not very sporting as I usually took the first shot while they were on the ground. The result was at least one duck for the pot. I hunted nearly all of that day, bagged four or five mallards, and became an avid duck hunter.

After that I hunted almost every morning and evening during duck season. Hunting ducks was my greatest desire. I would watch that hill from home, church, and school to see if ducks were circling and landing. If the ducks were present when I got home I would rush into my hunting clothes, grab my gun and run most of that half-mile to the top of the hill. If they were not circling, I would walk leisurely to my blind and simply sit and wait.

The attraction of those fields to ducks was the waste corn left behind by the pickers—some shelled and some whole ears. The fields to the east of the house also held some special attraction. Apparently it was because they were high on the watershed divide. Ducks would invariably feed there and ignore equally food-filled fields nearby.

There were hundreds of thousands of ducks around the neighborhood in those days. On some stormy mornings or evenings I could see flights of ducks stretched from horizon to horizon: a distance of five or six miles. Often they would continue to fly at this density for thirty minutes to an hour. Sometimes flocks would fly all day when "pushed down" by severe weather in the North.

By some unknown signal one flock would choose a field to investigate. They would break the classic "V" formation, slip and glide into a spiraling pattern, and then circle over the field investigating for food, enemies and whatever else ducks look for. If they did not like it they would regroup and fly on. If they did like it a few would flutter down and land, the rest would circle a few more times and then join their buddies on the ground. Often the circling and landing of one bunch would attract others and there could be thousands of ducks circling and feeding in a twenty- or forty-acre field. At a distance the flocks looked like small tornadoes in reverse. Sometimes I could look across the country and see three or four giant flocks going into different fields.

It truly was exciting to be beneath a flock as it was working the field in front and around you. The noise was a roar as they set their wings and held them rigid as they glided by. The air "whoosed" through their primary feathers. This sound was mixed with the quack-quack-quack of the females and the gentle rasps of the males. As they settled to the ground, or rose en-mass to change positions, there was a muted roar made by the hundreds or thousands of wings. Even now I can close my eyes and see the dark circles with the drooped wings and extended feet as they came in on a glide. As they neared the ground their short tail-feathers, which formed a white semi-circle on the drakes, were lowered to act as brakes as the birds hovered and touched down. Once on the ground they either waddled down the corn rows or, if in a hurry, flew up and forward a few feet and then dropped down again.

I soon learned that ducks working a corn field always feed into the wind. Apparently it helps them get airborne if they take off into the wind. Thus, I attempted to position myself up-wind from the flock. My hunting strategy was two-fold. The first was to wait in a blind. The blind often simply was an especially thick, and comparatively warm, bunch of grass or weeds in a fence row. Since the wind usually was from the northwest, and there were fences on the north and west sides of the field, this strategy often worked well. I also built several blinds out from the fence rows and closer to where the ducks actually landed and fed. My blinds were simple bunches of grass and corn stalks stacked together so as to form a good hide. I did get fancy enough to fill a "gunny sack" (burlap feed sack) with corn shucks for a seat in a couple of my better blinds. I would get into those blinds well before the ducks started flying and just wait for them to land and work toward me or fly over low enough to provide a good shot. In the morning the birds often started flying into the fields before sunrise. This meant that I often got into the blinds while it was still dark outside. In the evening I would get there as soon after school as possible and on the weekends I sometimes would spend a good part of the afternoons in the blinds.

The other strategy was to sneak up on them. I used this most often simply because I could not be in all of the blinds at one time and the ducks did not choose to land in the same location each time. I then tried to sneak close enough to get a good shot at the feeding or circling birds. If they were circling I would run to the likely landing spot while they were heading away and then freeze while they headed back in my direction. This was TRUE hunting that required an understanding of the birds and of the terrain—and a lot of stamina. Often I crawled several hundred yards down a fence-row, or up a ditch or corn row in order to get within shooting range. If the fence row or ditch ran close enough to the ducks, I would crawl right up to them. If it did not I would get as close as possible without scaring them and then sit or lie in wait and let them work toward me.

In the early or middle years when I was "meat-hungry" I would either shoot them on the ground or flush them and then shoot into the bunch when they got a few feet off the ground. The result of this last maneuver often was a limit of four out of one bunch. That accounted for my usual forty or fifty ducks per season while in high school. In later years I pass-shot while they were flying over me. That cut the harvest to one or two (or zero) ducks per group, but it was much more sporting and more rewarding.

The aesthetics of duck hunting probably can be understood only by its practitioners. In some respects it is the most elemental and aesthetically satisfying hunting sport. The non-hunter has trouble understanding why anyone would go out in the worst weather and risk frost bite just to shoot a duck. Indeed many times I nearly froze my fingers and toes and had to sit by the stove and endure the pain of thawing out. All I can say is that I found (and to some extent still do) a fundamental relationship between myself and the grandeur of nature when duck hunting.

Of all the places I have ever been, I found the duck blind among the most satisfying. Consider that you are in touch with the elements of the weather: low temperature, rain, snow, sun, wind as well as other forms of life. Feeling snow fly into your face, driven by a high wind while you sit among the grass on the ground or crawl on the ground toward the quarry is about as close to nature, and perhaps to man's core nature, as one can get. It is what our earliest ancestors did just to survive. That cold air and wind does not hurt. It just cleans the "junk" of civilization from your system. A distinct reward comes from just sitting in the hill-top blind on a sunny morning or evening and watching the sun rise or set.

Of the two times of day, watching sunrise from the duck blind was the more unique experience. On those clear mornings I saw lines of ducks or geese stretched against the lightening sky to the east, and heard the whistle of their wings as they passed overhead. Venus was a bright spot in the east that faded away as the sky lightened and the sun began to appear.

The sun sometimes was clearly revealed as it rose, but more often it was a red disk partially obscured behind the grey, then pink and gold, clouds. Eventually it peered into the mist-covered the valleys. The frost that covered the ground, corn stubble, and grass gradually would be revealed and slowly turned from a muted gray to a bright shimmering white as the sun's rays penetrated and bounced off the flakes. Then, almost suddenly, the light would flood the scene exposing the tree-lined ditches, the fence rows, and the surrounding fields and farmsteads in the distance. To view this scene was to be reminded of the promise of the day and of life.

Whereas ducks seen against the morning sky are thrilling, ducks seen against the evening sky are exquisite: the birds become moving black silhouettes against an orange sky mixed with changing yellows, grays, pinks and blues of the clouds. From the hills east of the house one can see across the valley to the next ridges two miles to the west. The horizon to the southwest and south is a bit farther, and to the southeast one can see across the Missouri River valley into the adjoining states. On a fall evening, usually about 4 PM, one could see bunches of ducks and geese, usually flying in the classic "V" formation, or some variation thereof, going north for the evening feeding. Often there were crossing flights of snow geese from the north returning to the refuge. Early in the evening birds were visible in all directions, but as the sun sank in the west it became difficult to see them against the eastern sky. At the same time they became more visible against the progressing sunset. From my usual vantage point I could see for several miles and watch each flock as it returned to the refuge for the night.

As darkness fell the whole scene became more peaceful as sights were replaced by sounds of the natural world going to bed. The wind would drop, and the occasional mooing cow or barking dog could be heard in the distance. At times the rapid "whish-whish-whish" of wings and an occasional "quack" came from above as the ducks passed overhead. By looking up one could see them silhouetted against the darkened sky.

The most memorable, and most beautiful, event happened early one evening as I sat on the ridge. Most of the sky was overcast with gray clouds, but there was a narrow patch of clear sky hanging above the western horizon. Just before sunset the sun passed into this relatively clear area to briefly light the country side before it slid into a lower bank of clouds. Suddenly its reflection off of the clouds cast a strong pink glow over the whole scene. At the same time a small flock of snow and blue geese flew directly toward me from the south. They were flying low and loosely bunched as if seeking a place to feed—going first in one direction and then another. As they turned to the east they were silhouetted against the dark grey of the eastern sky, but then the white geese suddenly, and briefly, were turned pink by the reflection from the western sky. The scene lasted but for a minute: pink birds against the gray sky. Then the sun dropped below the clouds, the geese returned to their black, white and blue, and passed overhead on their journey north. It was a brief moment of exquisite beauty that is unlikely to ever happen again—that specific match of sky, birds, and sun.

Ducks and geese have been  flying with the morning and

evening light for thousands of years, but now, unfortunately, this event can be witnessed by only a few. Drainage of nesting areas in the upper Midwest and parts of Canada have led to major declines in the population of some species—particularly mallards. The construction of new resting areas has resulted in dispersal of fall migrants over wider areas and in different local flight and feeding patterns than existed fifty years ago. In recent years, while on visits to the Homeplace during the fall, I still have seen beautiful sunrises and sunsets, but rarely sighted a flight of ducks.

MY BROTHER PAUL AND ME WITH MY FIRST (AND
ONLY) GOOSE  (circa 1954)

PAUL AND ME WITH A LIMIT OF MALLARDS
( November, 1971 in kitchen at the Home Place)

# SNIPE HUNTING

IT WAS A tiny- stream, only an inch or two deep and a few inches wide, that appeared as a seep spring from the hill side and then gently flowed about a hundred yards and gradually merged into a small grassy marsh at the bottom of the hill. The water ran clear between the border of sedges, grasses, and other small plants. Here was an oasis in the middle of a grain field: a miniature natural area in the midst of a man-made grain factory. The stream supported a rich diversity of aquatic life: algae, microscopic protozoa and related creatures, tadpoles in the spring and frogs in the summer. The most interesting, and probably largest, life form, though transient, was the jack snipe: a small  migrant shorebird that sheltered and fed among the grasses growing along the stream. Here it used its long bill to probe the soft mud for worms and whatever else snipes eat.

My main interest in the snipe was not its natural history, but the fact that it is considered by some a game bird and a particularly challenging target. As an avid hunter, I had successfully shot running  rabbits, flying ducks, doves, and quail and thus was not particularly awed by the stories I had read about the difficulty of hitting a snipe. My first attempt came shortly after discovering the presence of one feeding in the stream. It arose and with an erratic "zip-zip-zip" flew a short distance then settled again a few feet up the stream. I excitedly ran to the house,  got my shotgun, and ran back sure that I soon would kill my first snipe. As I walked along the stream, the snipe flushed ahead of me well within range. I took my time—it seemed an easy going-away shot—pulled the trigger and missed. I tried again, and missed again. Despite a few later attempts on others I kept missing. I never mastered dealing with the corkscrew-like flight pattern of the jack snipe.

Now I am thankful that I always missed. In subsequent years, while out walking, I either have periodically flushed snipe from along small streams or been lucky enough to watch them poking in the mud for worms. They are neither spectacular nor beautiful, but I now have a special affinity for them as each new encounter brings back pleasant memories of the first.

# THE MARSH

THE SOUTHERN TWO thirds of the west edge of the Home Place was bottomland that bordered the adjacent Wildcat Creek. The soil, very rich Marshall Silt Loam, was the best on the place, but the southern half of the bottomland supported a well established marsh-swamp. My father viewed the marsh as unproductive land, but I viewed it as paradise. The northern end of the marsh was covered with cattails, "ripgut," and other grasses and sedges. These were home for red-winged blackbirds, song sparrows, jack snipe and other birds. They also provided part of the raw materials for the mud and grass houses built by muskrats where the standing water was deepest. On one occasion I watched the rats building their house. One would select a large reed and gnaw at its base until it fell. Then he would pick it up in his mouth and start a labored swim toward the unfinished house. The animals mixed and piled grass and mud until they had a partially hollow dome nearly three feet in diameter, about two feet high, and with walls a foot thick. An underwater entrance was built into one side. This, their home, provided shelter for the litter of young and protection from predators and the weather. In winter the water froze solid, but the animals presumably were warm within their lodge and able to live on stored grasses. Their only danger was farm boy turned trapper, a practice I followed a couple of winters.

I actually caught two or three muskrats, took the skins and stretched them and perhaps sold one or two for fifty cents each at a local market. In this adventure I was aided by reading a magazine titled *Fur, Fish and Game* which provided instructions on trapping, skinning, and preparation of the skin. One of the skins I fashioned into a cap. I took a cloth cap that had exterior ear flaps, cut the dried and partially cured skin into pieces that fit the flaps and hand-sewed them onto the flaps. When the ear flaps were up the fur was on the outside, but when I pulled them down the fur was next to my head. It made a very warm, if not particularly attractive, cap for hunting and doing the chores.

There were several large open pools of water about two-hundred feet south of the muskrat houses. In the early spring the pools often filled with flocks of blue-wing teal and mallards, and an occasional, relatively rare, pintail. Later, after the ducks had gone north, the frogs and toads deposited masses of jelly-like eggs. The eggs hatched, the pools became alive with wriggling multitudes of tadpoles and the tadpoles grew into adults. On warm summer nights these clans of amphibians would gather on the shore and start singing. Their seemingly labored, but lovely and mysterious calls could be heard for a great distance. Often I lay in bed and listened to them come floating through the inky blackness.

From the pools to the road (now County Road 140) at the south end of the marsh stretched grass, a few large trees, and great carpets of what we called marsh marigolds (actually a marsh sunflower, _Bidens sp_). When the marigolds first began to bloom they looked like stars against the "sky" of green, but within a few days the "sky" would be masked with a solid sheet of rolling yellow blossoms. When a southerly breeze blew, the flowers took on the appearance of a gentle yellow sea, rolling forward, ever forward, to be stopped by greater sea of green.

A strip of grass and meadow extended east from the marsh. This was choice nesting cover for birds. Among the more unusual inhabitants was a family of pheasants. Although I seldom saw the cock pheasant, my first sighting was most memorable. In his bright coat of reds, greens, and blues embroidered on a dull brown base he resembled a living gem strutting about in the morning sun. Later I once saw the hen come strutting out of the grass followed by a family of eight fluffy brown youngsters. They would lag behind, but then suddenly rush up to her in a group to share in a tidbit of food or receive instruction in pheasant matters. But she then stepped back into the grass and suddenly they were gone. This was a rare occurrence because pheasants never became well established on farms near the Home Place. In some years, particularly after the advent of the Conservation Reserve Program Soil Bank, there would be several. But local participation in this program was sporadic, and as the cover was converted back into row crops the population again fell due to the lack of nesting and winter cover.

During the first years on the Home Place the marsh was one of my most favored places. I visited it at all times of the year watching ducks and other birds in the spring, tadpoles, frogs and muskrat in the summer, ducks again in the fall, and trapping muskrat in the winter. But,a few years after moving to the Home Place my father cut down the trees and drained the marsh. I actually cried and scolded him for doing so. On the other hand the corn and soy beans that grew here helped pay my way through college to earn a degree in Wildlife Conservation and provided my parents with a financial pad to pay for the farm and keep them in old age. Very little of the marsh now remains. The land occasionally floods, but the underlying tiles and drainage ditch assure that it drains  quickly. All of the former inhabitants are gone—including the "marigolds." Not a single one remains. The future of this piece of land is uncertain. Possibly, with the aid of the USDA Wetlands Restoration Programs, it could be restored. However, over the passing years significant amounts of soil have washed onto it from the hills upstream, thus restoration may no longer be feasible. One consolation is the wonderful memory of this place and the events that occurred there. It is sad that across the nation we continue to lose such wetlands at a high rate and that current weak legislation and economically dominated aesthetics of many landowners does little to stop that loss.

# THE CREEK

A PORTION OF Wildcat Creek was located across the road from our house on the Home Place, less than two-hundred feet from our front door. This creek served a drainage of about twelve square miles located mostly to the north and west. The headwaters of the main branch started in the Heck's pasture three miles north of our house. Before it reached our house it was joined by another branch from the northwest. A few yards south of our barn it received another major branch from the west. For most of its length it ran a natural course, but, for reasons unknown to me, the section near our place had been straightened by dredging in the 1920s or 30s. Here it ran straight for nearly a mile. The channel had been cut through deep loess soil, thus the sides and bottom were soil, not rock or gravel characteristic of mountain or glacial streams. The bottom was firm yellowish clay except in pools where it could change to a few inches of mud. The banks were uniformly fifteen to twenty feet high on both sides and nearly straight up in many places. The only slopes were formed where the bank had given way and piled into the stream bottom.

The top of the creek channel was about forty feet across, but the stream itself averaged only two to four feet across, a few inches deep, and ran with only a moderate current. Due to runoff from adjacent fields the water rarely was clear although in winter, and occasionally after a long dry spell, one could see minnows darting about. After a heavy rain the water became full of silt and the creek then flowed nearly bank full. Once or twice a year, after a real "gully washer" (three inches in one hour) the stream would overflow and flood the bottom lands south of our house. Between the creek and the road, there was a strip of woods and weeds about eighty feet wide that extended for four-hundred yards north and south. The creek, adjacent banks and this wooded strip formed the focus of many of my boyhood activities.

During my eighth summer, I found a then relatively large pool ("hole") in the stream that had been formed by water washing past an old stump embedded in the bank. The true dimensions of the hole were only about six feet wide, fifteen feet long, and perhaps three feet deep in the middle. We called this Louie's hole because it was located on Louie Kunkel's land about thirty feet downstream from the single plank bridge that formed part of Louie's path from his mailbox to his house. The pool was populated by a mixture of small bullhead catfish, the largest of which probably was ten inches long, and a few carp that may have reached fifteen inches and two pounds. At this location one side of the bank was fairly flat, grass covered and gently sloping to the water—a perfect fishing and swimming spot.

I do not remember how or why I decided to start fishing there. My granddad Loucks and Dad had taken me fishing down in the river bottoms the previous summer so I guess I had simply learned the rudiments and set out to try fishing on my own. I purchased a fishing set from the hardware store in Craig. It was a green line, a hook and a cork bobber wrapped on a red wooden frame. My pole was a piece of left-over board from one of the construction projects—about six feet long by one inch square. After digging some worms, which I stored in a tin can, I proceeded to catch a few small bullheads and thus became an independent fisherman. After that first successful trip I spent part of many days at that fishing hole. It was less than a fourth of a mile from the house. Mom still was suffering effects of the fever, thus I was free and unfettered to go, accompanied by dog or cats, as I wished. My catch usually was small in number and size, but even small bullheads are edible and delicious when fried.

I sometimes took a bucket so that I could bring them home alive for close observation or to dump into the horse tank. I had to dress my catch, but Mom would dutifully cook them for supper and if there were enough Dad and Mom would each get a bite or two.

Gradually my fishing and exploring extended upstream and downstream, but there were no other fishing holes of that note. This one remained my center of activity for several years and one time attracted the attention of the neighborhood. One summer day, when the water became very clear, I saw several small (they looked large at the time) carp swimming in and above the hole. I excitedly reported this to Dad and he reported in turn to David Painter who owned a long trammel net—commercial fishing net. Shortly, he, Dad, Louie and several friends set the net around the hole and by splashing attempted to drive the fish into it. I do not recall much success—perhaps a few small carp, but most probably were so small that they swam right through the net.

I left Louie's fishing hole behind with the discovery of neighbors' ponds stocked with more exotic fish such as blue gill and bass. I can not remember the last time I fished there, but still recall the mink that came almost to my feet while I sat very still fishing on one of the later trips and the dead beaver I found on the ice that covered the pool that subsequent winter.

The fishing hole also served as a swimming hole. It was long enough to allow a few dog-paddle strokes up and down its length. My friends and my cousin Steve Jackson and I used it several times—unknown to our parents. For some reason I had bouts with flu-like illness several summers in a row. Likely it was contacted from the dirty water of the creek while I was swimming. The neighbor Freed's hog lot, located barely one-half mile upstream on a tributary, washed into the main stream one hundred yards above the hole. Typically the tributary water was far dirtier than that of the main stream and undoubtedly full of bacteria. That I did not become very ill no doubt was due largely to good luck and a fairly strong constitution.

Over the intervening years the stump that formed the turbulence which created the hole washed out and the hole disappeared. Today all traces are gone. Still I sometimes marvel at the temporal coincidence of the existence of that fishing hole and a small boy—actually two as my brother also caught his first fish there. It too was only a small bullhead, but it made him into a fisherman. The last time I fished with him he caught a forty-five pound King salmon.

As a graduate student in1961 I collected fish from the creek and found  healthy populations of several kinds of minnows as well as the usual sunfish and bull heads, but that was before the advent of the heavy use of farm pesticides. Now the pesticide load in the water must be very heavy since most of the runoff comes from cultivated grain fields. I would be surprised to find many fish in the stream today.

On-the-other-hand beaver returned to Wildcat Creek in the late 1960s and currently several active colonies are present. The individual dams wash out or are abandoned from year to year, but beaver have been present here for at least the past thirty years. Their survival clearly has been helped by the corn fields that border the creek.  It is not unusual to find areas in which the mature corn stalks have been sheared off and dragged into the beaver ponds. This annually renewed source of food  no doubt compensates for the relative shortage of small trees, a food source which usually is depleted in one or two years. The ponds formed by the beaver dams in turn have attracted wood ducks and king fishers, and in the spring often are used as resting areas for blue-winged teal and an occasional pair of mallards.

The narrow strip of land between the road and the creek made an ideal exploring and "hideout" area. It was covered with a mixture of small trees, weeds, and coral berry bushes. This was, and still is, excellent rabbit and bird habitat. In my earlier years I built a "camp" across the road from the barn. My best construction was a tree house made by nailing four tree limbs in a rectangle between four adjacent small walnut trees. On top of these I nailed boards crossways to make a four by six foot platform about five feet above ground. I next contrived a frame above the platform which I overed with feed sacks that I stitched together. Thus I had a covered tree house that served as the centerpiece of my camp and which was hidden from the road. To this I added some stools, a camp fire pit, and a couple of tin cans to be used as pots. It was a wonderful world of my own: constructed and managed entirely by me.

The fire pit was used for cooking franks and marshmallows. However, on one occasion Virgil Miles, my neighbor to the south, and I killed a pigeon in the barn with our BB guns and then tried to cook it for lunch. We dressed the bird, filled an empty coffee can with water and proceeded to boil the bird. We cooked and cooked, but the bird remained so tough that we could not even bite through the breast. In the end it was donated to the cats.

In the spring a large patch of wild Sweet William (blue phlox) and purple violets bloomed in the woods near the camp. I always picked Mom bouquets of both. To this day Sweet William is a favorite flower and the sight of them in the spring brings back happy memories.

In the winter the wooded strip provided an excellent place to hunt rabbits. In addition to a few brush piles, there were two abandoned hollow iron bridge girders lying on the ground near Louie's path. These served as rabbit hideaways, but they also provided a potential source of rabbit for a hunter. First I would get down on hands and knees and look in to see if a rabbit was inside. If so, stomping on the top of the girder was usually sufficient to flush the animal. I shot several using this approach, but often the rabbit came out the "wrong" end and escaped into the brush.

Following a snow storm the area would become crossed by

numerous rabbit trails. After several days the trails became packed and formed into temporary rabbit "highways" converging on the girders or brush piles. If the snow persisted, the trails became dotted with droppings and yellow patches of rabbit urine. Also the hungry rabbits gnawed the bark off the small trees or bushes. All were sure signs that rabbits were present. The foxes knew this. Often their tracks also could be seen leading to the girders or brush piles.

It was very pleasant to walk through this area on a moonlit night when snow was on the ground. It was quiet with few signs of life—the rabbits were hidden by the shadows even though their trails and tracks were clearly visible in the moonlight. Judging from the tracks it was evident that foxes and coyotes had been about, but they were far too shy to permit detection.

Today the creek and wooded strip remain. The woods grew to include several nice walnut trees. However the REA decided they were getting too large and close to the power line and some were sprayed in the 1980s—possibly indiscriminately. The spray obviously killed some trees clear back to the streambanks. Today many of the trees are dead. None-the-less, these dead trees attract woodpeckers, and the living ones are heavily populated with a variety of birds including bluebirds, white-breasted nuthatches, chickadees, Harris sparrows, and the more common cardinals and blue jays. The woods remain only because the strip is too narrow to farm and if the trees were cleared the land would rapidly erode away. Only luck of location has preserved it, and only by happy coincidence was it located across the road from our house.

# THE BLACKBERRY PATCH

THE SECTION OF land west of our house contained many wooded fence rows and several streams bordered by trees. Two streams joined in the middle of the section. One started a mile west in Bud Nauman's pasture, crossed under the road and wound its way almost due east where it joined Wildcat Creek below our barns. The other arose in Harold Judy's fields a mile to the northwest, angled south-southeast and joined the first about four-hundred yards behind Louie's house. The joining formed a "Y," the interior "cup" of which faced the west. The streams themselves were rather small, carrying only one or two inches of water within a width of one foot or less during most of the year. However, these small permanent streams lay at the bottom of natural channels that were ten to fifteen feet deep, and fifteen to twenty feet wide at the top—the result of periodic heavy run-off from the surrounding fields. The property lines, which had been laid out in strict linear fashion, crossed just to the west and south of where the streams joined. This arrangement formed within the cup a patch of land two or three acres in size bounded by streams on two sides and a wooded fence row on the west. Other fence rows joined from the south and west. Due to the depth of the stream channels, this patch was inaccessible from Louie's fields which lay to the northeast and south. As a result it had lain fallow for many years and gradually reverted to a mixture of forest, mostly black walnut trees, and a heterogenous under story of weeds, coral berry, and black berry vines.

Aside from wooded creek banks and a few osage orange hedge

rows, this patch formed one of the few, and actually one of the largest, pieces of "wild land" in the community. Not surprisingly, it was excellent wildlife habitat and was well populated with fox squirrels, song birds, a few quail and many rabbits. The surrounding grain fields contributed to the food supply and the thick brush provided excellent cover. The stream banks were used as travel routes by wandering raccoons and foxes. On rare occasions a mallard or a few wood ducks would take advantage of a small pool formed at a meander in the stream. In the 1960s beavers moved in, dammed the creeks in several places and provided resting places and shelter for broods of wood ducks that nested in some of the large maple trees along the streams.

The wildlife attracted the local hunters: notably me and a few neighbor boys. I visited this area numerous times each winter for several years in search of squirrels, quail, and rabbits. To this day, some fifty years later, I can draw a reasonably accurate map showing the location of the thickest blackberry bushes. In later years, when hunting had become less of a motivation, I visited it as a place simply to be out of doors. For two or three years, when I was in high school, several of us would meet on Sunday afternoon for group hunts. Usually we would pile into the Rosier's jeep and go off looking for rabbits. In those days, we kids had virtually unlimited access to every field in the neighborhood. Often we ended up in Louie's blackberry patch. Typically we reduced the rabbit population, though sad to say only rarely kept a rabbit to eat. Usually they were left for the foxes.

Our motivation was more that of a friendly outing rather than gathering food or counting trophies. On one occasion one of us killed a rabbit with a shot gun while part of the group was off hunting another part of the patch. I took the dead rabbit, set him upright in a life-like pose, then wandered over to my friend Larry who was hunting with a single-shot 22 caliber rifle. Gradually we hunted back in the direction from which I had come. As we approached, Larry cried, "There is one sitting over there," and then shot it. He never knew the difference.

This area also served as a camp site. One Thanksgiving or Christmas vacation, while I was home from college, my brother and I decided to go winter camping in the Blackberry Patch. We packed some canned beef stew, bread, bacon, eggs, and likely some water for coffee. Also we borrowed a skillet and kettle from Mom. We did not have either sleeping bags or air mattresses. We each took a couple of old blankets, some feed sacks to stuff with grass for mattresses, and either my home-made feed sack tent or a tarp from the garage. Apparently I had bought an army surplus backpack for somehow we got all the stuff together and carried over there. Our half mile trip to the Patch was uneventful. We gathered a lot of downed wood for a fire, ate early, and because it got dark early, soon settled into our beds. About 2 or 3 AM we both were very cold—so cold that we got up, started a fire and sat out the rest of the night. Breakfast was earlier than we had planned because the hot food was needed to warm us. We then broke camp and headed home at first light. That was my one and only winter camping experience—great fun only in retrospect.

I regularly returned home on Thanksgiving and Christmas vacations and always wandered back to the Blackberry Patch to collect a rabbit for Dad who really enjoyed fried rabbit—a taste which I shared. For several years, when home on holiday, I visited the patch with binoculars and camera. The Patch gradually became a retreat to visit simply for enjoying wildlife, thinking, and listening to the bright autumn or winter days. Being located in the middle of the section the Patch's only sounds usually were those of the birds, the chattering of the fox squirrels, or occasional call of a quail seeking its brood mates. Sometimes a flight of snow geese, passing overhead against a clear blue sky, would notify me of their presence with plaintive calls. On one evening, under a greying eastern sky, I watched a lone mallard cross over the creek and flutter down into a beaver pond.

I admit to always carrying a shotgun, although in later years it often was unloaded and served primarily as a prop. I am not sure how the local neighbors would have responded to seeing a "stranger" walking through the fields with a camera and binoculars just to bird watch or putter, whereas a hunter with a gun was a common sight. The Blackberry Patch was still there the last time I visited, but the two fence rows joining it from the west and south had been removed. I then decided not to go back because I suspect that the memories of this place are far more valuable to me than knowledge of its present condition.

# THE TEMPLE

THE LATE MARCH snow storm was unexpected. The day before, while on a visit back to the Home Place, I had watched muskrats feeding on new spring grass and listened to red-winged blackbirds singing in the warm sun. This morning I left tracks in the snow as I walked north up the road in front of the house. I stopped at the bridge to listen to the water trickling beneath it and observe the hairy woodpeckers as they silently hopped up the walnut tree to the east. In the overgrown blackberry clump beyond the bridge the Harris sparrows warbled as they socialized and greeted the day.

I walked on up the road to Carl's abandoned farmstead. The driveway, once bordered by two rows of tall catalpa trees, now was overgrown with grass. The old house was still standing, but with broken windows and flaking paint. Up the hill and beyond the house the once magnificent white-sided, green-roofed main barn now was a pile of boards and shingles lying in disarray atop the brick basement that once sheltered cows. At the north end of the collapsed barn a row of partially buried stalls was visible through the dimly lighted doors of the debris-covered basement. A few bits of leather harness and still intact bales of rotting hay covered the floor.

The south end of the barn still stood: a sloped-roof shed supported by the peeled red cedar poles that formed its uprights. Most of the shed sides were gone, but the tin roof was intact. The floor was covered with well-composted hay, a rusted license plate, fragments of machine parts, and an old black and yellow feed sign. The opening on the east side gave a view of the grassy field that led down to Wildcat Creek flowing off to the southwest between steep tree-covered banks.

The new snow had formed a thin covering of purity outside, but a few flakes had blown into the shed where they had mixed with the hay. The only sound was the wind rustling through the row of pine trees in the windbreak along the north side of the property. As I stood peering into the dark recess under the old barn I became aware of a movement at my feet. Looking down, I saw a small gray and white bird, a junco, scratching and searching for bits of food among the decayed hay. I stood still so as to not disturb him as he, paying little attention to me, hopped about my feet. A gust of wind blew some flakes of snow off the roof and across my face and ruffled his feathers, but he continued undisturbed. After all he had as much right to this place as I. Perhaps in this decaying work of man the junco was simply Nature's expression of the certainty that in the end she will slowly reclaim and abolish all our works and make us equal. We humans who think in calendar years, argue about our affairs, exclaim about 100 year-old antiques and get excited about 2000 year-old ruins forget that our species has existed but for a tiny fraction of earth's history. We forget that Nature has wiped out far larger creatures than we, buried their remains in the mud, and sealed them in stone for millennia. No doubt the same will happen to us, our buildings and our varied pieces of technology. Perhaps the junco was there to remind me that his tiny kind had been here longer than mine and that some day, in our absence, they still may be calmly feeding among the remains of our decaying works.

The junco probably knew that, and his quiet going about his business may have been his way of showing that even among the rubble of civilization the simple folk can find food, that both of us could feel the wind that has been here since the earth was formed, and I could be reminded of mortality on one hand and of the assurance that my present being is connected with both the past and the future.

I stayed but a few minutes in the old shed. The spell was broken when the junco decided to look elsewhere for breakfast and flew off into the weeds. I soon satisfied my curiosity, my attention wandered and I walked on down across the pasture to seek other lessons.

# Map of land sections surrounding the Home Place
## showing houses, Bellevue School and New Liberty Baptist Church
### (1950's through 1994)

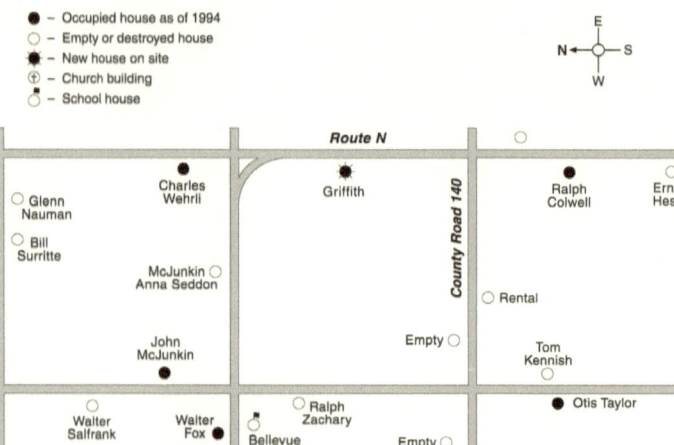

● – Occupied house as of 1994
○ – Empty or destroyed house
✸ – New house on site
⊕ – Church building
⌂ – School house

N ←◇→ S (E / W)

**Route N**

County Road 140

Glenn Nauman ○

Charles Wehrli ●

Griffith ✸

Ralph Colwell ●

Ernest Hester ○

○

Bill Surritte ○

McJunkin ○
Anna Seddon

Rental ○

John McJunkin ●

Empty ○

Tom Kennish ○

Walter Salfrank ○

Walter Fox ●

Ralph Zachary ○

Bellevue School

Empty ○

Otis Taylor ●

Ike Painter

Howard Dearmont ○

Randall ○

David Painter ●

John Meyer ○

Don Taylor ○

Oscar Siekman ●

Mary Judy ○

Gary Bruntmeyer ○

Tone Wright ○

Carl Nauman ○

**Jackson Home Place** ■

Theota Miles ○

? ○

**Ironwood Road**

Strough Place ○

Bill Horton ○

Ed Doan ○
Leroy Freed

Loren Pender ○

Harold Cromer ○

Rental ○

Earl Judy ✸

Richard Miles ●

Louie Kunkel ○

Lloyd Rosier ○

Blaine Buetzer ○

New Liberty Church ⊕

Johnny Mann ✸
Jim Rosier

●

Rental ○

Lee Stoff ●

Leonard Freed ●

Harold Judy ○

Bud Nauman ○

Orville Sharp ●

Pruitt ○

Marlin Smith ○

Shaky Showwalter ○

Taylor ●

Bill Stone ●

# REFLECTIONS

AS I CLOSE this story, thoughts of thankfulness and reverence for the wonderful childhood that I experienced are mixed with thoughts about the many changes which have occurred in the land of "Cows" over the last sixty-plus years. To these are added speculations and concerns about the future of this region.

Although I have traveled enough to experience great mountains, oceans, jungle, and the tidy country sides of parts of Europe, I still find "cows country" very beautiful. But, I feel that some of the good things which contributed so much to the quality of life in the land of "Cows" have peaked and now are disappearing or gone. I do not know if that feeling simply reflects the longings of an old man trying to preserve memories of an idyllic childhood or is an objective judgement based on experience and travel. If it's the latter, current residents, who number among this country's finest and "best-hearted" folk, might take issue with my judgement.

The most obvious change is the disappearance of many farmsteads that once occupied these rolling hills. The economic structure of modern agriculture has resulted in larger, but fewer, farms. In some cases the bigger farm simply reflects the need or desire to enjoy the social recognition and sense of accomplishment of being a "large operator." But, indisputably, economic pressures (increased costs and many years of stagnant commodity prices) have pushed farmers toward farming "bigger" in order to ensure financial security. The farmer of today can produce far more than the farmer of the past, but, paradoxically, it requires a much larger farm to support an economically viable unit today than it did in the past. Larger farms have led to, indeed required, larger equipment whose operation is impeded by small fields. The result has been a gradual switch from general mixed animal and grain farming to predominantly mono-culture farming of corn and soy beans. The interspersed, relatively small, pastures, grain and hay fields common in the 1940s or 1950s have been replaced with a uniform landscape of relatively large grain fields.

Along with this change, it appears that relatively little— arguably too little—attention is given to controlling soil erosion, preventing pollution of streams by soil runoff and pesticides, providing wildlife cover, or simply beautifying the landscape with trees and grasses. Terraces are becoming more common, but many fields still lack them. Unfortunately, the benefits of terraces too often are compromised by other practices. Wooded fence rows and wooded or grass strips along streams have been removed to accommodate big equipment and squeeze another tillable acre from the landscape. Grass-covered field borders are the exception rather than the rule. In a few places corn has been planted in the roads! Few of the streams have effective buffer strips, and grassed waterways are rare. In contrast, in flat Champaign County, Illinois over seventy percent of drainage streams are bordered with grass cover strips.

It seems that each time I return to the area I see another bare spot where a house once stood, or another pile of trees where a fence row has been pushed out and piled along a stream. It is understandable why so many unoccupied farmsteads have disappeared. Unused barns and unoccupied houses are expensive to maintain. After my father passed away, my mother kept the barns in good condition for several years even though they were not used. But, eventually it was necessary for her to move to town. Although she wanted to keep the farmstead and maintain the buildings it was not economically feasible. Today the two barns are approaching collapse. Still, the "clearing mentality" seems all too common. In many places removed fence rows have not been replaced with terraces or other erosion control procedures. Perhaps it is as easy to push the thoughts of long-term consequences out of mind as it is to push a tree off a hill.

In the long run, success or failure of the farmer hinges on efficiency which is determined, in part, by soil productivity. As the soil deteriorates it will require more and more expensive management practices to wrest a profit from it. The local "hill-farmer" must compete with those who work more fertile soils in other parts of the nation or world. Marginal land-use practice is but one, yet in some localities an important one, of the many factors which have led to the depopulation of rural areas across the nation. It has been, and I fear may continue to be, one important to the land of "Cows" and much of the rest of Holt County.

I cannot predict the future with any certainty, but I foresee, if current trends continue, this region to be dominated by excessively eroding large grain fields and relatively deprived of small song and game birds, trees and even people. In planning parlance it is questionable whether current practices are sustainable in that portion of the county which lies outside the Missouri River valley.

Whereas some landowners will pay little attention to this concern, others will strive to leave future generations with land and a landscape that provides enjoyment and value in addition to money in the bank. These folks are committed to the idea of conservation and to leaving future generations a stable and enjoyable countryside. They will switch to low-till or no-till cultivation, plant cover strips along the ditches, streams and terraces, leave a few fence rows and forested areas, build a wetland, set aside a corner of the farm for wildlife, and perhaps even build a pond. I am not sure, but I suspect that future generations will need and appreciate the joys of seeing and hearing birds in the trees and grasses provided by these folks. Those who live in the growing cities may even come here to live or just to walk, bike or drive along country roads to see and enjoy the efforts of the "better builders." Ironically some of this land may become more valuable for recreation than for farming. It is noteworthy that today some advertisements of farmland for sale in this region list the presence of forested, or Conservation Reserve Program acres, and the opportunities for "Good Hunting." In some regions, the value of recreational land is increasing at a rate faster than the value of good farm land.

Less obvious, but perhaps more significant than changes in the landscape, are changes in the population density; a trend that has been ongoing for many years. The 1870 population of Holt county was recorded at 15,510. At the end of 2006 it was slightly under 5000. The population in the immediate area surrounding the Home Place, as is illustrated by the accompanying map, declined by over fifty percent during the last fifty years. In the early 1950s fifteen people lived along the one mile portion of Ironwood Road where the Home Place is located. Today there are three. And they are not farmers. Two of four local community church buildings are completely gone, and one stands empty. Even the large brick school house is empty and decaying. Both the structures and institutions have disappeared. Sadly, most communal memories of the people that built, maintained and occupied them also are lost.

The future of some small towns in the area is problematic. Decreases in the rural population are reflected in relative desertion of the main streets. Small towns in Holt County are plagued with empty stores, sagging buildings, and vacant lots where thriving businesses once stood. Most communities have lost their grocery stores. Three once served Mound City, but now there is only one. Two drug stores have been replaced by one, and its relatively bare shelves suggest that it may be struggling. Even the two hardware stores that once fronted opposite ends of the main street are gone. Fortunately the lumber yard survives and also provides a basic line of hardware. On the bright side, a few chain businesses have appeared. Two national fast-food franchises and a pizza parlor provide additional options for eating out, but on some nights of the week it can be a challenge to find a good full meal in the area. A chain variety store moved in few years ago, and while it offers some items that the drug store and grocery store cannot, it also competes with both for sales of many of the more profitable items.

Both the social and economic conditions that surrounded and influenced my childhood were unique to that time and place. However, changes similar to those that occurred in the Bellevue community and Holt County have been repeated across much of rural America—particularly the Midwest. Sagging barns, decaying houses and empty store fronts in small towns are a common sight in this part of America. In many respects the stories in those varied communities are similar to those in "Cows" country. How these small towns adjust to these new situations will vary. Some will disappear, others will hang on, and a very few will flourish. Those located either near larger cities or in scenic areas may thrive as homes for commuters or seasonal residents. The others will continue to struggle and, unless they attract new industry or find other ways to increase their population, will pass into memory.

As I bring these recollections to a close, I again am reminded that the social- and economics-induced disappearance of all traces of once prosperous and beautiful farmsteads from the locale of "Cows" clearly attests to the transiency of our influence upon the landscape. On a personal level it is sobering to realize that so too my "monuments" will someday disappear into history. For the "old" person the message is to do the best with the time left, and for the young the message is to consider well what you want to do with your life. There are choices of whether to "enjoy the time we are given," or to concentrate on "building monuments" so that we will be remembered, or to serve others so that their lives might be more enjoyable. My experience with "going after the cows" suggests that most people likely will not leave many noticeable or significant monuments! On the other hand, those who are endowed with the necessary "gifts" should recognize their good fortune and perhaps commit to leaving those rare monuments. And I suggest that most of us can serve others in small, if not major, ways.

A parting thought is the recognition of the richness of my experiences growing up in this place. Perhaps that recognition is not unusual in that we all experience, to some extent, unique childhoods. None-the-less I know that a special combination of time, place, and people made my childhood the wonderful experience that it was, and provided the special memories that are mine. I truly wish for other kids some of the joys of "going after the cows."

# ABOUT THE AUTHOR

Gary L. Jackson is Professor Emeritus of Veterinary Biosciences at the University of Illinois at Urbana-Champaign. He grew up on a farm in northwest Missouri, graduated from the smallest high school in the state, and then attended the University of Missouri at Columbia, earning degrees in Wildlife Management and Zoology. He completed a PhD in Animal Sciences at the University of Illinois. Remaining at that institution, he taught physiology in the College of Veterinary Medicine for 33 years. His research on the brain and reproductive system took him across North America and to parts of Europe and Australia for professional meetings and sabbatical studies. The author of more than 100 refereed articles published in scientific journals, this is his first contribution to popular writing.

www.ingramcontent.com/pod-product-compliance
Lightning Source LLC
Chambersburg PA
CBHW020244290526
45784CB00003B/1099